THE BLACKMORE VALE PATH

BY

EDWARD R GRIFFITHS

A SIX DAYS WALK THROUGH HARDY
COUNTRY AND OVER THE BLACKMORE VALE
WITH DETAILED MAPS AND SKETCHES

INCLUDES A GAZETTEER OF PLACES VISITED

BOOK THREE

BY THE SAME AUTHOR

THE STOUR VALLEY PATH - ISBN 0 9519376 1 8

"...the book is a gem which anybody..will add quickly and gratefully to their bookshelf".............Dorset Life

THE CRANBORNE CHASE PATH - ISBN 0 9519376 2 6

"...the anecdotes..and passionate descriptions will delight even those familiar with the Chase"................Western Gazette

"...combining exciting local colour with meticulous route information"..........Greenlink Countryside Guide

ST JAMES', MILTON ABBAS - PAGE 20

First Published - 1995

ⓒEDWARD R GRIFFITHS

ISBN   0 9519376 3 4

Published by Green Fields Books
13 Dalewood Avenue
Bournemouth BH11 9NR

THE BLACKMORE VALE PATH

CONTENTS

THE BLACKMORE VALE PATH

ROUTE MAP

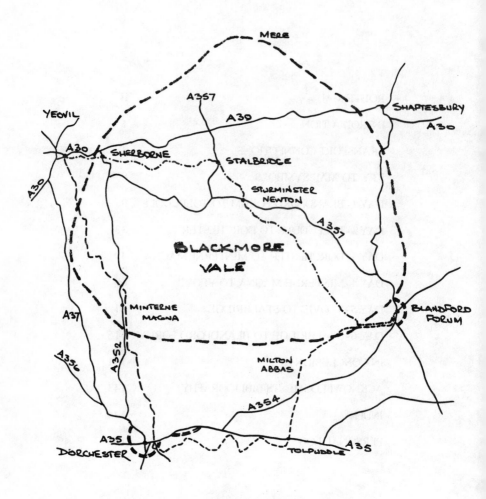

ROUTE 1: Blandford Forum to Dorchester - shown as:

ROUTE 2: Dorchester to Yeovil - shown as:

ROUTE 3: Yeovil to Blandford Forum - shown as:

THE BLACKMORE VALE PATH

INTRODUCTION

First of all, you will have noticed a change from the format of the first two books in the Green Fields Books' series of guides, The Stour Valley Path and The Cranborne Chase Path. Originally, the intention was to use a large, clear print to make it easier to follow on-the-move than the usual guide books. However, the large print meant that I had to leave out some of the useful and interesting information which I had gleaned in my researches and which I would have liked to share with those of you who are following in my footsteps. This book has a new style print which is just as clear but it is a little smaller, so there is a lot more detail about the towns, villages, churches and the landscape.

Now, I must explain the title of this long-distance path. When I decided to explore the area to the West of Blandford Forum, (having walked much of its North Eastern and Northern environs for The Cranborne Chase Path and The Stour Valley Path) my long-time appreciation of the low, warm hinterland of the Blackmore Vale led me to plan a new route which would show off the best that Blackmore Vale has to offer.

Blackmore Vale (or Blackmoor as it appears on the Ordnance Survey map) is not confined by Parish or Parliamentary boundaries and it has no precisely defined area. In fact, it proved impossible to get any local authorities to commit themselves when I asked, "What are the boundaries of the Blackmore Vale?" The foremost authority on Blackmore Vale has to be Fanny Charles, Editor of the Blackmore Vale Magazine, that eagerly awaited free weekly magazine which is distributed throughout, and beyond, the Vale. I am grateful for her help in defining the virtually undefinable, basically as follows: "With Sturminster Newton at its centre, the Blackmore Vale extends to just beyond the chalk ridge above Mere in the North. It runs to the Cranborne Chase escarpment in the East and down to Bulbarrow Hill in the South. In the West, it is enclosed by the ridge which includes the village of Buckland Newton and extends up to Sherborne".

Being a "Vale", the area is, by definition, low lying and surrounded by high ground so the best introduction would be from this same high ground, looking into the Vale. Now, a walk around the nearest ridges would be at most 30-35 miles and could be accomplished in 2-3 days comfortably. This would hardly be a long-distance walk in the already 'time-honoured' manner of the previous two walks. So, I decided to extend the new path to embrace some of the most enticing downland on the perimeter of the Blackmore Vale, ending up as far South as Dorchester (the County town of Dorset - in Hardy country) and then to turn Northwards to its North-West corner at Yeovil (actually in Somerset) and Sherborne, finishing with a two-day hike straight across the middle of the Vale back to Blandford. In this way, I have been able to lead you to some of the grandest ridge and valley walking in this beautiful part of Dorset and to incorporate the Souther extension into a triangular walk around and across The Blackmore Vale.

Anyway, this is magnificent countryside and our walk takes us through ancient forests and over chalk downland, across flat plains of Oxford Clay and into many beautiful villages and historic towns. Take your time with this journey. Modern life needs the occasional period of calm and this is the place to get it. Breathe in the fresh breezes on the high downs and feast your eyes on the luscious landscapes spread out in front of you. Stand still awhile and just watch the birds, butterflies, insects and animals (wild or well-bred).   Enjoy the intoxicating, oxygen-filled and pine-scented air in the forests and the balmy breezes of the meadows and downs.   Feel a part of the Dorset which fired the talents of Thomas Hardy and William Barnes.

As much information, historical and legendary, as it is possible to fit into the space available, has been squeezed in but, if you don't have enough time to linger very long in the towns and villages on "The Blackmore Vale Path", promise yourself a return visit to really get to know them - they'll amply reward your interest.

The journey is divided into 6 Days of between 8 and 13.1/4 miles and each Day is further broken down into short Stages, each of which has a detailed map right next to the explanatory and informative text.   The whole walk can be undertaken in a 6-day week or spread over a few weeks or even seasons.   You don't even have to do the Days in number order if you don't want to.   Each Day is so unlike the previous one or the next one, that it doesn't matter about continuity and, however you decide to break up the journey, you're in for a veritable feast of Dorset.

This circuit of Blackmore Vale has a major market town at all of its three corners, Blandford Forum, Dorchester and Yeovil, whilst the entire route is blessed with small and beautiful villages, each with a character all its own.   There are magnificent stately homes which are still home to the same families as hundreds of years ago. There are fine ridge walks and soft, green valleys with clear, chalk streams and rivers. There are connections with famous authors, probably the most famous Elizabethan adventurer, a great scientist and a man who saved millions of lives by giving the world the means to combat smallpox.   There is a lovely model village built by an intolerant lord because the old cottages offended his view and his plans for a lake. There is a strange and wonderful Giant carved on the hillside above a lovely village founded around an ancient Abbey. and, whilst on things ecclesiastical, we visit town and village churches, some big, some small, but all with their own particular appeal.

The section on "Transport Connections" shows where cars can stop either to drop you off or to stay all day awaiting your return - or to stay near a bus stop at the end of your Day's walk so that you take an early bus to the beginning of your Day and walk back (my own preferred method because it doesn't matter how long you take).   All bus routes which are closely approached during each Stage are also shown so that you can break off at a convenient Stage before the Day's end if you're tired.

The beginning and end of each Day is on a major bus route, either Wilts and Dorset or Southern National.   You can obtain copies of the relevant timetables from Tourist Information Centres at Blandford Forum, Dorchester, Sherborne and Yeovil (all on The Blackmore Vale Path) or, if you are staying on the coast, from T.I.Cs in Poole or Bournemouth.

Now, what about Rights of Way.   What must you do and what must you not do?   If you've already bought The Stour Valley Path and/or The Cranborne Chase Path, please forgive me for repeating the following information about Rights of Way and Countryside Acts but everybody has to be aware of their obligations and rights:

1.   Signposting and Waymarking - The County Council only has to erect signposts where a public Right of Way leaves a tarmac road.   Also, the Council has the power to waymark paths where the route is not obvious - but it doesn't have to.   Stiles and

2

gates have to be maintained by the landowner where they cross paths - "to the standard of repair required to prevent unreasonable interference with the rights of the persons using the Footpath or Bridleway" - Section 28; Countryside Act 1968.

2. Paths Through Fields - If a path *follows the edge of* a field, the surface must not be ploughed or disturbed. The law requires a minimum width of 1.5m for a Footpath and 2.5m for a Bridleway at the edge of the field. If the path *crosses* a field or enclosure, the path must be reinstated within 14 days of ploughing to a minimum width of 1m for a Footpath and 2m for a Bridleway - Rights of Way Act 1990.

3. Obstruction or Loss of Path - The County Council recommends that, when faced with an obstruction on the correct route e.g. lack of stiles, gates or exits from fields, you should make a slight deviation and report the obstruction to the Rights of Way Section of the County Council. Such obstructions are illegal under Section 137 of the Highways Act 1980.

4. Bulls in Fields - A bull may not be released into a field or enclosure crossed by a Right of Way unless it is less than 10 months old or, if older, accompanied by cows or heifers. Unofficially, eleven cows is the minimum safe number of cows per bull or it may still have the energy to chase you.

Now, what should you take on this journey? I would always recommend hiking boots or at least a good, stout pair of shoes with profiled soles when you are walking anywhere on hills, tracks or Bridleways. You should carry suitable waterproofs in your backpack just in case you get a sudden downpour - and this IS England. You will only need Ordnance Survey Landranger Maps Nos. 194 and 183 for the whole route. A simple compass could be useful, but not essential because I point out targets if there is any doubt which way you have to go at any time. As for food, why not take a few sandwiches, some fruit and a flask. There's nothing like a simple picnic on a breezy hill or on a bench outside a church or on a village green.

Before you go, allow me to say a few personal words. This is working Dorset with real people going about their work and leisure and we must respect everyone's right to privacy, peace and quiet as we approach and pass through. It isn't a Country Park, built for our amusement - but having said that, there is more to see and to enjoy as you pass around and across the Blackmore Vale than could ever be reproduced in any Country Park. Oh, yes, and another of my foibles - Village shops. These little shops, which are in grave danger of disappearing altogether because of the proliferation of out-of-town hypermarkets, are the life-blood of remote villages and they need our support. The corner shop provides more than food, drink and hardware to the local area. It provides a valuable social service as well but, unable to compete for price with the conglomerates, many have been forced to close. If you pop into every village shop (alright then, some of the village shops) which you pass on these walks and buy something which you would have bought at the supermarket next week, you will be helping to preserve this vital service for just a while longer. Tell them I told you to call - every little helps.

One last comment - We're all being propelled into Europe at an alarming rate and, from 1st Oct 1995, it is illegal for shops to sell pints, pounds or ounces. If this applies to my book, I'm in trouble. You will notice that I still think in feet, yards and miles. I'm going to try harder next time although I'm not convinced that *you* can picture a 185 metres hill any more than *I* can. To me, 600 feet can be visualised but, if I get into terrible trouble, you will come and visit me inside, won't you?

THE BLACKMORE VALE PATH

TRANSPORT CONNECTIONS

The following lists indicate possible parking places but, it is of paramount importance that you cause no obstructions to gateways, openings or tracks or to the progress of farm vehicles on country lanes. The Blackmore Vale is a lovely area and you will be welcomed but - *you are only a guest!*

Buses are mostly Wilts and Dorset or Southern National whilst some of the local, rural services are operated by smaller companies. Relevant Timetables can be obtained from Tourist Information Centres or direct from Dorset County Council in Dorchester for the Blandford, Dorchester and Sherborne areas and Somerset County Council in Yeovil for the Sherborne Yeovil and Dorchester areas. Check timetables for route times and, don't forget, not all routes are operated every day of the week.

DAY 1

BLANDFORD FORUM TO TOLPUDDLE

STAGE	STAGE MILES	CAR STOPS	BUS ROUTES
1	0	Blandford Car Parks	X94, 111, 139, 181, 184, 185, 186, 190, 237, 303, 311, 322
	0.25	-	Blandford St Mary 139, 184, 185, 303, 311, 322
2		nil	nil
3	3	Lay-by, Broadley Wood	nil
	4	Winterborne Stickland	40, 111, 311, 322
4		nil	nil
5		nil	nil
6	6.75	Milton Abbas	111, 324
7		nil	nil
8		nil	nil
9	10.25	Dewlish village	111
10		nil	nil
11	13	Tolpuddle	123, 184, 185, 187, 188

DAY 2

TOLPUDDLE TO DORCHESTER

STAGE	STAGE MILES	CAR STOPS	BUS ROUTES
1	0	Tolpuddle	123, 184, 185, 187, 188
2		nil	nil
3	2.25	Lay-by on Puddletown Lane (for 1)	nil
	3.25		Puddletown 40, 111, 123, 184, 185, 187, 188
4	4	Puddletown Woods Car Park	nil
5	6.75	Lower Bockhampton	100, 104 at Bockhampton Xroads
6	6.75	ditto	ditto
7	7.75	Off St Georges Road, by By-pass	125
	8.25	Fordington	95, 125
	8.50	Dorchester Car Parks	7, 40, X68, 100, 104, 107, 109, 111, 123, 184, 186, 187, 190, 211, 212, 216, 238, 338, 799 in Dorchester

DAY 3

DORCHESTER TO MINTERNE MAGNA

1	0	Dorchester Car Parks	ditto
2/4		nil	nil
5	6	Godmanstone with care	216
	6.25	Nether Cerne thoughtfully	216
6	8.25	Cerne Abbas	216
7	8.25	Cerne Abbas	216
8		nil	nil
9	11.50	Minterne Magna - not in Private Car Park	216

DAY 4

MINTERNE MAGNA TO YEOVIL

STAGE	STAGE MILES	CAR STOPS	BUS ROUTES
1	0	Minterne Magna - not in Private Car Park	216
2	2.25	Hermitage, nr village hall	216
3	4.50	nil	211, Totnell Corner
	4.75	Leigh, off main street, with consideration	211, 212
4	5	ditto	ditto
	5.50		211, 212 and BR 123 to Yeovil at Chetnole
5	7.25	Yetminster	200, 212, BR123
6	7.50	ditto	ditto
7		nil	nil
8	10.25	Yeovil Junction Station	55, 80, BR145
9	11	nil	55 at Barwick (Mowleaze)
10	12.25	Yeovil Car Park	4, 7, 15, 28, 40, 57, 58, 68, 69, X94, 190, 200, 212, 216, 243, 338, 631, 705 in Yeovil

DAY 5

YEOVIL TO STALBRIDGE

1	0	Yeovil Car Park	ditto
	0.50	nil	Yeovil Pen Mill Station 57, 80 and BR123
2	1.25	Estate road	nil
	1.75	Lay-by on top road	Bradford Abbas 55, 200
3	2.50	Wyke Lane, carefully	ditto
4	4.75	Estate roads	nil
	5	nil	Lenthay Road 57

DAY 5 CONTINUED - ON PAGE 7

6

DAY 5 CONTINUED

STAGE	STAGE MILES	CAR STOPS	BUS ROUTES
5	5-6	Sherborne Car Parks	7, 228, 57, 69, X68, X94, 181, 190, 200, 211, 216, 243, 631, 705, BR145 in Sherborne
6		nil	nil
7	8	Haydon, near Park gate area - 1 only, carefully	nil
8/9		nil	nil
10	11	Stalbridge Weston, with care	244
12	12.50	Stalbridge Car Parks	7, 15, 28, 58, X94, 190, 235, 630, 631, 799 in town

DAY 6

STALBRIDGE TO BLANDFORD FORUM

1	0	Stalbridge Car Parks	ditto
2/3		nil	nil
4	3.75	Sturminster Newton Car Park	48, X94, 190, 236, 237, 241, 243, 303 various stops
5	4.50	Sturminster Mill -if visiting	X94 on A357
6	5.25	Broad Oak	nil
7	7	Okeford Fitzpaine - with care	40, 190, 237, 303, 312
8	7	ditto	ditto
	8	Okeford Hill Picnic Area	40
9/10		nil	nil
11	10.75	Lay-by Broadley Wood	nil
12		nil	nil
13	12.75	nil	Blandford St Mary 139, 184, 185, 303, 311, 322
	13	Blandford Car Parks	X94, 111, 139, 181, 184, 185, 186, 190, 237, 303, 311, 322

KEY TO MAP SYMBOLS

ROUTE	
FOOTPATH OR BRIDLEWAY ARROW	
SIGNPOST	
HEDGE	
WIRE FENCE	
WOOD/IRON FENCE	
STONE/BRICK WALL	
STILE	
GATE. LARGE/GATE. SMALL	
BRIDGE OVER STREAM	
DECIDUOUS/PINE TREE	
SPECIFIC BUILDING	
GROUP OF BUILDINGS (SCHEMATIC)	
STREAM/RIVER	
EMBANKMENT/HILLSIDE (Arrow points down)	
OVERHEAD CABLES	
MILES FROM DAY'S START	
ADJOINING MAP NUMBER	

DAY 1 - INTRODUCTION

BLANDFORD FORUM TO TOLPUDDLE

This first stage of your journey leads you across and around high grazing and arable fields enclosed by ancient hedgerows, through magnificent woods and forests and beautiful, calendar-worthy villages. This is Dorset at its best - full of wildlife, strewn with flowers and with fine, downland breezes and superb views. And you're never alone. You're in the company of skylarks, yellow-hammers, wood pigeons, crows, rabbits and, of course, the dairy herds which occupy this intimate landscape as they did in Thomas Hardy's day. Also, if the time of year is right and you are walking circumspectly, you'll see migrant birds and roe deer.

You start outside the parish church in the historic market town of Blandford Forum and head out, over high fields and across gentle, grassy valleys to the ancient villages of Winterborne Stickland, Milton Abbas and Dewlish (all of which were mentioned in the Domesday Book) on your way to Tolpuddle. This is beautiful country and you should have your camera ready.

	STAGE	MILES	TOTAL MILES
1.	Blandford Forum to Beech Clump	1.00	1.00
2.	Beech Clump to Quarleston Down	1.25	2.25
3.	Quarleston Down to Winterborne Stickland	2.00	4.25
4.	Winterborne Stickland to Charity Wood	0.75	5.00
5.	Charity Wood to Milton Abbas	1.25	6.25
6.	Milton Abbas to Fishmore Hill	1.25	7.50
7.	Fishmore Hill to Gallows Hill	0.75	8.25
8.	Gallows Hill to Dewlish	1.50	9.75
9.	Dewlish to Milborne Wood	1.25	11.00
10.	Milborne Wood to 113 Triangulation	1.00	12.00
11.	113 Triangulation to Tolpuddle	1.00	13.00

DAY 1 - STAGE 1

BLANDFORD FORUM TO BEECH CLUMP

We start The Blackmore Vale Path at the memorial water pump outside the Church of St Peter and St Paul but, before you set out on the first Stage of the first Day, here is the first lesson of the whole journey.

Blandford Forum is the administrative centre of North Dorset and it has been a market town since a grant from Henry III. It appears as *Bleneford* in the Domesday Book and the name is most probably derived from the British - *Blaen-y-ford* 'the place in front of the ford' although Hutchins (into whose monumental work we will be dipping from time to time) seems to prefer the Saxon - *blaegna ford* 'the place where gudgeon were seen'. The town prospered in its situation on the Great Western Turnpike road between London and Lands End which was begun in 1755.

This memorial pump is dedicated to John and William Bastard, the builders who were responsible for rebuilding the town after the disastrous fire of June 4th 1731 which started in a tallow chandler's house on the corner of Salisbury Street. During the rebuilding, this new church was completed in 1739, replacing the original which was destroyed in the conflagration, whilst the Corn Exchange was built behind the Town Hall in Market Place having a vast elliptical roof supported on five, ornate cast iron 'principals springing from piers'.

Now, we'll begin - Walk along Market Place to the far end and leave down West Street, passing the "Three Choughs" and the "Crown Hotel" on the RH corner. The old milestone against the iron fence opposite shows that it is 17 miles to Dorchester (by road) and 104 to Hyde Park Corner. However, continue down West Street, passing the Tourist Information Office on the LH corner of the Car Park entrance next to the Toilets, and looking across to your right to see the fine beech-clad slopes of 'The Cliff', the woods on the edge of Bryanston School's grounds, beyond the flood plain and the River Stour. Recent flood defences now prevent the river from invading the town in times of deluge as it did in past times. Past the telephone box and the bench on the LH pavement, cross the river bridge and keep straight on into Blandford St Mary when the road turns left to Poole and Dorchester opposite the stone arched entrance to 'Bryanston School and Arts Centre'.

Cross to the tree-bedecked green opposite, with the "Stour Inn" down on your left, and then cross over to the pavement on the RH side, following the stone wall, past the smart house with the columns either side of the door, to the 1st right corner. Turn right into New Road (only a track on the 1937 O.S. map),signed to 'Bryanston 1/4', and cross over to the gate on the left after the twin rows of cottages, just before 'The Old Riding School'. Follow the direction of the Footpath arrow on the post, over the edge of the RH slope and keeping 30 yards to the left of the solitary tree.

Keep on up the hill, over the stile in the hedge and up to the far LH corner at the top of the next field where another stile puts you on a concrete farm track. Instantly, turn right and go through the gate with the faint, painted Bridleway arrow into the next field. In a matter of feet, go through the next gate and follow the wire fence on the left along the top of this next field with the valley down on your right. This is a wide, grassy path which is confined between wire fences, the LH one being on a bank. Keep on up, with a few hawthorns in the fences, through a gate across your path, with Beech Clump just ahead.

THE BLACKMORE VALE PATH

DAY 1 - STAGE 1

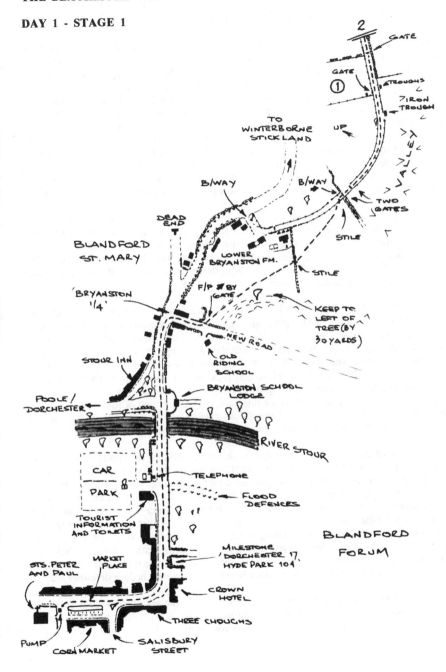

BEECH CLUMP TO QUARLESTON DOWN

Whilst strolling along this grassy track, overgrown with docks and nettles, occasionally looking back towards to the Blandford Brewery of Hall and Woodhouse in the river valley and contemplating the thirst quenching beverages which emanate from its worthy portals, I was aware that I was getting closer to a cuckoo whose call I had been hearing for some time. At this point, let me say that I was walking alone and into a Northerly breeze (unusual for that time of year) so that any sounds of my approach would be carried away behind me. Anyway, the sound got louder and louder and it was clearly coming from the left one of two chestnut trees immediately facing the end of the straight track. I stood quietly near this tree for several minutes, trying to see the cuckoo but failing but, just as I was about to leave, the cuckoo took off and flew deeper into the woods and I then heard him, or her, calling from further away. At the same time, a buzzard looped overhead so I hope the cuckoo kept its head down.

Now, having turned to follow the edge of the wood on a narrower footpath with elderberry bushes and sycamores on the edge of the Beech Clump, the path soon begins a slight descent and comes to a gate across the path which leads you into a sloping field with two farmhouses and a brick and flint barn down on your right. Past the trough at the top of the field, stay up high until you reach the gate into the woods facing you, with a painted blue arrow on the gatepost.

This is Old Warren Plantation where a grassy path takes you through the woods for about 1/4 mile amongst mostly pines and beeches which are full of bird song. After cross-tracks, the path begins to ascend again, at first dense and overgrown (in summer) but then wider and steeper where the trees begin to thin out into an airier section. Suddenly, you are out of the woods, through a gate in the wire fence and into an uphill field. Just halt for a while and pick out the farm gate in the fence at 11 o'clock from where you are standing (with the chimneys of the Quarleston Kennels to the right of that next gate). Head for this gate, next to a clump of four new trees, with another painted blue arrow. Go through the gate and follow the wire fence on your right, bearing slightly right towards the facing gateway when your fence runs out.

You will have noticed some smart red-brick houses beyond the fields down on your left as you crossed and, as you go through this gateway, the track leads down to them on the left. You go the other way, past an concrete area on your left, past barns on your right and ignoring any tracks which turn off right. You then emerge into an open area with gates all around - right, left, behind and facing you. The clearest way is the tarmac lane which goes off to the right - ignore it, whilst making a mental note that this is the way you'll be coming home at the end of the very last Day of this journey. Also ignore the painted arrow on the facing gate. Instead, bear left, through the gate with another painted blue arrow, onto a wide track with grass up the middle, a wide RH verge at first and with beech and hawthorn hedges on either side.

After a RH stile in the hedge and a LH gate, go past the gate across your path with another painted arrow and continue, ascending slightly now, with a higher hedge on the left and the first part of a beech wood on your right.

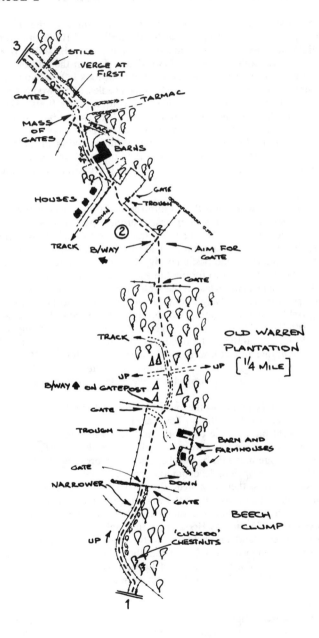

QUARLESTON DOWN TO WINTERBORNE STICKLAND

Enjoying the stroll along this woodland path with grass up the middle, this is an excellent opportunity to compare the blank sterility of 100% pine forests with the more enlightened mixed pine and hardwood plantations. Broadley Wood, for this is where you are, has both. At first, it is all dense pine on the left and beeches on the right but it becomes blended better later. For now, look left and you will see that the forest floor is dark, dead and covered with pine needles. The woods on your right are more open, lighter and with a selection of vegetation on its floor. There is no bird song on the left because there is nothing living there for the birds to eat but the trees on your right are full of song (if you arrived quietly, anyway) because there are insects, caterpillars, beetles and other creepy things living in the branches and on the trunks of these trees. Thank goodness the Forestry Commission now recognises the sense in growing mixed woods, even if they are slightly less production-line-friendly.

Anyway, follow the winding path and join the main track which comes in from your right. Keep straight on, now on a firmer surface, past a grassy track which goes down on your left, to the end of the forest track. Go through the opening to the right of the barrier into the forest entrance and out onto the Winterborne Stickland road. Turn left along the verge and past a lay-by which is big enough for about four cars and then cross over to the right to follow the safer side, to the RH corner. Go through the smaller of the last two gates on the right, with the painted blue arrow, and enjoy the high, open fields as a change from the woods. Keep to the RH hedge across the first long field to the next gate. Go through into the next field on a more distinct path and with the hedge still on your right. This is now skylark and yellow hammer country. You can hear them all around you when it's warm and sunny. The next gate is another small one and, at last, there is a more official-looking Bridleway arrow disc actually nailed to the gatepost. Go through this gate into the third field and enjoy the views across the panorama of fields to the distant ridges of the Dorset coast.

Keep going, slightly uphill, to the end RH corner gate with a Bridleway disc, and go through onto a tarmac T-junction. There are fine views all around from this gateway. Now, go straight on, into the downhill lane between high hedges. There is a well-trimmed lawn with some fine shrubs on your right, followed by a stable and paddock, whilst the banks are mounted by beeches and sycamores and harts-tongue ferns grace the steep sides. An opening leads up to Sycamore Down Farm on your left, followed by steep steps, whilst there is a steep drop beyond the bank on your right. After a fern wall on the left and past two thatched cottages facing some large cedars over the flint wall on the right, you emerge onto Clenston Road, Winterborne Stickland. *Wintreburne* in the Domesday Book, the village takes its name from the Saxon *Sticel-land* 'steep, sloping land. and belonged to the church of Coutance in Normandy until England had so many wars with France that they decided to sell it, or mortgage it, to the Abbey of Milton during the reign of Edward III. The church is in Perpendicular style and was rebuilt in 1716. The West tower holds three bells dated 1622, 1626 and 1670.

Now, turn right and follow the village green round to the left, admiring the fine new sign on the corner and the well-kept, bench-bedecked lawn with the 'winter bourne' running through it. Go up the hill, past the fence of Dunbury School, past the gate to 'The Old School House' on your left, and past the turning down on your right.

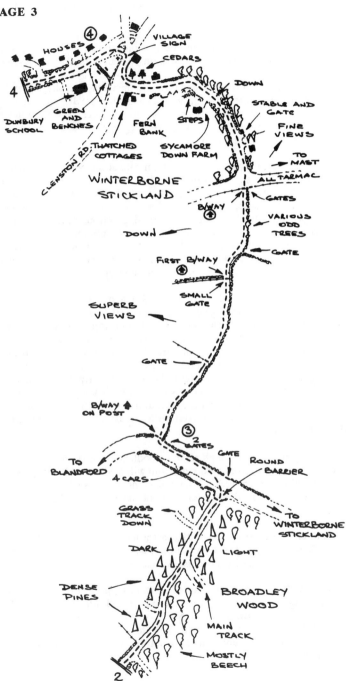

DAY 1 - STAGE 4

WINTERBORNE STICKLAND TO CHARITY WOOD

On your way up this lane, you will have to 'tack' from side to side to keep yourself in view of any oncoming traffic but you'll soon see the Bridleway post ahead of you, just before a signed Footpath goes back on your right under some sycamores.

Cross to the LH side of the lane and turn into the track to 'Valley View Farm' - not the house - past the Bridleway sign and through the small gate where you are asked politely to "Close gates properly and Keep dogs to heel". Not too much to ask, is it? Follow the track between the LH hedge and the RH wooden fence past some barns to where the track turns right into the yard.

Keep straight on, though, through the farm gate at the end of the facing hedge with a DCC arrow on the post. The direction of this arrow is very accurate and you should follow it, across the valley at an angle towards the far RH corner of the field. When you arrive in the corner, with the fenced hedge across the valley and the sparsely bushed fence along the high edge of the field, go through the small gate into the next steep field. On this gatepost, you will see, not only another DCC Bridleway arrow but the first of several 'Jubilee Trail" arrows which you will see for the next couple of fields. These are part of a marked trail to commemorate the 60th jubilee of the Ramblers Association in 1995 but we aren't concerned with its route today.

Keep to the rising footpath next to the RH hedge to the top of the field and go through the fence-protected gateway into the next large field. Here, you join a wide path going to the right but this soon turns left on top of a raised track bisecting two open fields and heads off towards the woods on the other side. As you stroll across these fields, take time to enjoy the fine, long views which spread out on your left from South East to North East as the LH field drops down to the Winterborne valley. Reaching the other side of the field, the path bears right (with more arrows on the facing fence next to a distorted elderberry) and leads you to a gate next to a short piece of wooden fence. Go through the gate into the wire-fenced wood and, if its spring or early summer,, you will find yourself with a mass of bluebells or foxgloves on both sides of the grassy path.

This is a lovely stroll through mixed woodland and, shortly after you join a wider track which comes in from your right, you will find yourself among some ancient, and vastly spreading, beech trees. When you come across such old and revered trees, it's difficult not to think, albeit briefly, about our own mortality. Right, that's long enough.

Keep on, enjoying this forest walk, past a left descending track and a right grassy track. This is Charity Wood, part of the vast Whatcombe Wood which is divided into four named areas - Charity, Oatclose, Whatcombe and Milton Park Woods.

In Hutchins 'History and Antiquities of Dorset', he records that, about 1793, "three pairs of roe-deer *Capreolus Cervus* were introduced into the Milton Abbey Woods by Lord Dorchester, one pair from the North of England, and the rest from America, and so well did the situation and climate suit them, that their descendants are now to be met with over a considerable tract of country". On the way out of these woods, I came across a very junior member of the dynasty - but I'll tell you about that later.

16

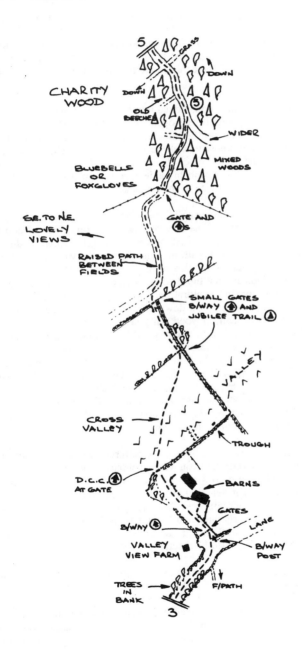

CHARITY WOOD TO MILTON ABBAS

Whilst enjoying this forest stroll, it almost felt as if I was in one of my favourite places in the whole of England - Whinlatter Pass Forest in the Lake District. Both have mixed woodland, both have these winding tracks because of the steep hillsides and both have steep-sided cuttings against the trackside where ferns, euphorbias and myriad wild flowers grow. And both have the wonderful smell of pine in the summer warmth.

Anyway, back to the plot. You have now moved into Milton Park Wood where there are more bluebell and foxglove plants in the open, fertile floor of the forest and, as the track becomes flinty, with grass up the middle, you may notice a lot of bloody-nosed beetles in the track. You know what I mean, don't you? They're about 1/2 inch long, very shiny black and, if you touch their front end, they'll deposit a blob of red ink that looks like blood. This is probably a defence against predators as the ink may well have an offensive smell or taste to their attackers.

Now, continue, past a LH track and another RH grass track and, uphill slightly, join a track which comes in from the right. This now becomes long, level, gravel and easy with a left sweep and the start of a descent. At the very next right sweep of the main track, look left and you'll see a narrow path descending into the woods. There is a blue painted arrow on a tree, pointing into this path. (There are also two arrows on a tree before this path which indicate that the Bridleway also continues straight up and down the main track). On my first exploration, I missed all three but the quickest way is down the narrow path, bending on a downhill slope, until it emerges back on the track on the other side of this hairpin wood. If you want to stay in the open, just follow the main track down around a right sweep, a left bend, another right sweep and a left hairpin to find the narrow path coming out of the woods on your left about 100 yards down the track. If you kept to the right, you will have passed a blue-painted arrowed path going off to the right at the left hairpin. This was part of the route of Lady Caroline Damer's Carriage Drive of the mid-1800s which took her from the High Lodge of the Milton Abbey estate through her woods to the Winterborne valley beyond and the 1937 Ordnance Survey Map still showed this path to be the same size and classification as all of these other forest tracks.

Well, now we're all together again where the narrow path rejoins the main track, keep on down the track for just a few yards and you will see another blue painted arrow on a tree on the right. This leads you onto a narrow, steeply rising, loose path. Go up this path and you soon have a wire-fenced field on the right, tree roots in your path and a grassy track going off to your left opposite a field gate. This is where I saw the baby roe deer. I was alone and fairly quiet and I don't think his mother had told him to be frightened of heavy-booted walkers. I had time to take off my back-pack and take two photographs before he decided he'd better go and find his mum.

At the top of this narrow path, still with fields on your right, start a steep descent to the forest track at the bottom where you will find a wide gate across the track on your left and confirmation Bridleway and Jubilee Trail discs on the gatepost. Turn right and follow the left hairpin bend between mixed trees again. On a right, uphill bend, you leave the forest and continue, past a paddock on your left and again on your right, to join the wide, hedge-lined tarmac lane to Milton Abbas, passing a selection of houses on the way.

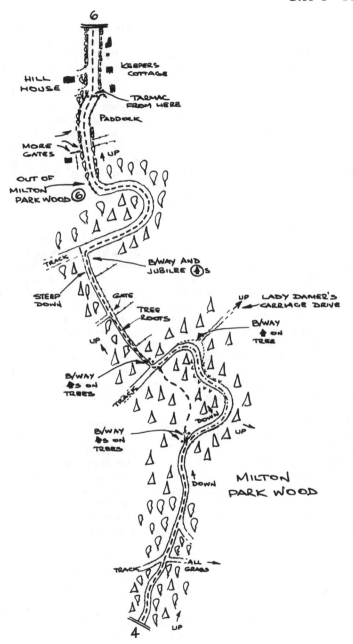

6

KEEPERS
COTTAGE

HILL
HOUSE

TARMAC
FROM HERE

PADDOCK

MORE
GATES

UP

OUT OF
MILTON
PARK WOOD 6

TRACK

B/WAY AND
JUBILEE S

STEEP
DOWN

GATE

TREE
ROOTS

UP LADY DAMER'S
CARRIAGE DRIVE

B/WAY
ON
TREE

UP

B/WAY
S ON
TREES

TRACK

DOWN

B/WAY
S ON
TREES

UP

DOWN

MILTON
PARK WOOD

TRACK

ALL
GRASS

4

UP

MILTON ABBAS TO FISHMORE HILL

At the end of the lane, with the Bridleway post on the RH corner, carefully cross over the Winterborne Whitechurch road to the pavement outside the Victorian cottage in Catherines Well opposite. Keep straight on, past the telephone box at the lay-by on the right and the houses on your left until you are opposite a Bridleway post pointing down the road on your left. Turn left and aim for the bottom RH corner house with the gravel drive. Turn down the path between the RH wire fence and the LH hedge, following this descending path round two bends, down some worn wooden steps with a laurel hedge on their right, past a big beech in the path and out onto the pavement by the child barrier, having negotiated a wooden chicane at the exit. Turn right, with the cemetery gates opposite, and follow the pavement down with trees on the slopes over on your left. A Footpath goes up into these trees but ignore it. Keep on down, past Dunbury First School on the RH bend with the "Hambro Arms" opposite, next to the defunct Methodist Chapel. At the brick house past the Chapel, the grass verges open up to front-garden size on both sides of the road in front of a succession of identical rendered and thatched twin cottages.

These cottages are a lovely feature of the village but they are only here to suit the whims of fashion which demanded that a gentleman's country house be surrounded by a park with a fine lake. In the mid-1700s, Joseph Damer, later Lord Milton, began a policy of allowing the cottages of Milton to fall into disrepair so that they could be demolished. The village had grown up in the valley around the Abbey and it spoiled his view and his plans for a park. At the same time, between 1763 and 1769, several roads which served the village, including the main road to London, were closed by legal order. Many legal devices were used by the villagers to delay the inevitable destruction of their homes but, by 1791, the rows of new cottages which stand today were completed. Lord Milton may have moved his villagers but he couldn't beat nature and his planned long lake did not materialize because the water supply was insufficient to cope with the natural drainage of the surrounding land. All he got is the small lake which you will see today at the foot of this hill.

Mideltune in the Domesday Book, Milton Abbas gets its name from its association with the abbey and also from the Old English - *mylen-tun* 'village with a mill'. King Athelstan founded a monastery here between 937 and 940, dedicated to four Saints - Mary, Michael, Sampson and Bradwalader. The old Abbey church was destroyed by fire in 1309 and the existing Abbey replaced it although the nave was never completed. Oh, well. Get walking again - but only as far as the Church of St James which stands opposite the almshouses of 1779. The church, in a Gothic style, was also built by Joseph Damer for the 'new-villagers' and it was dedicated in 1786 by the Bishop of Bristol to whose diocese Dorset belonged at that time.

Now, with head spinning with dates and names, head off down the hill, past or via the Cream Teas Shop and the Old Forge. At the bottom, the road on the right leads to the Abbey and its grounds but you need to go left and follow the pavement all the way round, past hidden houses, a long barn and drives to streamside cottages on your left, to the next T-junction with Lower Lodge on your right. The main road goes left to Dorchester (11 miles) but go up the hill ahead of you instead, past the Lodge's iron-fenced garden, between tree-lined banks and with the Milton park flint walls on the RH side. Trudge up this hill until you have passed 'Fishmore Hill Farm' entrance on your left.

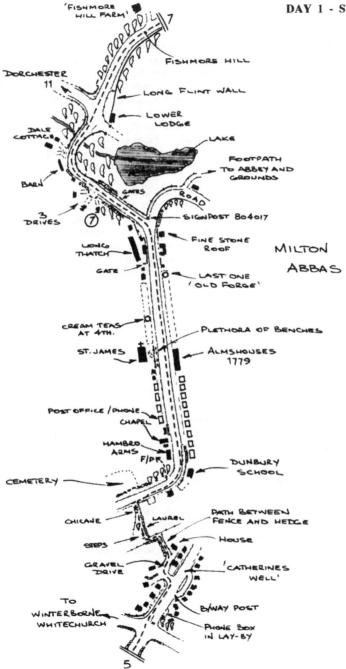

FISHMORE HILL TO GALLOWS HILL

The next farm entrance on your left may or may not have a Bridleway sign but the RH farm gate is the one you want to take you up the concrete yard, with a large barn on the right and smaller barns on the left, to the next farm gate with an unusual chain latch, into the first field of many to come between here and Tolpuddle.   Through the gate, keep straight on up the edge of the field, past two ash trees in the hedge, to another gate which leads you into a high field with a hawthorn hedge on your right. From this high spot, there are fine views over massed, hedged fields as far as the coastal ridge.   This is typical 'enclosed' field country although some later fields are larger than they would have been originally.   Field enclosures began as far back as the 15th Century (although most are 16th Century), so some of these hedgerows are really ancient and have been home to birds and small mammals ever since.

However, passing a gate in the hedge, you arrive in the corner of the field with a gate in the wire fence across your path and a small valley to go down and up on your way to the next gate, after you have passed the remains of a bank and hedge on your left and a cattle trough in the RH hedge.   Through the gate, you emerge in a huge, open field where you join a flinty track with grass up the middle as it comes from the next gate and runs down towards a deep valley.   At the end of this field, go through the gate in the hedge, with the track, and descend into a hedged gully which is lined with honeysuckled hawthorns and beech hedges.   At the bottom of the track, a rare sight greets you - an official Bridleway arrow on a marker post which confirms that you have been legal since you left Fishmore Hill, even though there have been no markers all the way.

Cross the lane, with Long Close Farm on your left and a sign which shows that this farm is home to the Milton Flock of British Charolais Sheep.   You may have met some already but, if not, you will soon.   Go through the gate nearly opposite which has another Bridleway arrow and follow the flinty track up the side of the valley, steeply, to the pair of gates at the top.   Go through the RH of the two gates (no arrows) and follow the LH hedge slightly uphill, past a trough and a gate, and then begin a slight descent to a small iron gate tucked into the far LH corner of this field. The track may be overgrown with long grass and hogweed if you're here in summer or it may have been cut down and left.   Whatever, I wish you good luck as you enter a narrow, fenced-in alley leading to another iron gate in the right corner of this next field.   Through the second gate, turn left and follow the wide, grassy track along the LH hedge which has a few elderberry bushes growing in it.   The straight-on path after the last iron gate would take you up to Gallows Corner - a junction of five Bridleways but far too confusing to keep you safely on the right track.   So, keep on going, downish/levelish along a low valley, to the far LH corner of this field.   Through the gate in the corner, you arrive onto a grassy track with a hedge on your right.   Keep to this track, keeping a lookout for browsing bunnies - sorry, I mean rabbits.

DAY 1 - STAGE 7

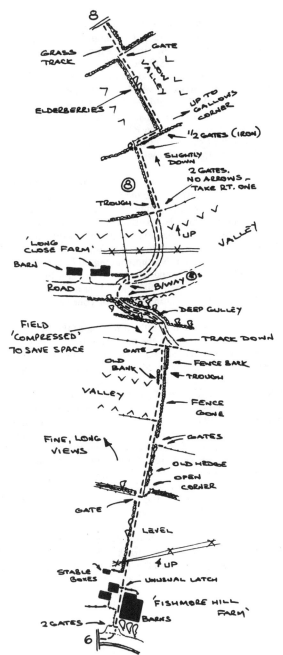

GALLOWS HILL TO DEWLISH

At the end of the hedge, there is a large oak tree on the right, just by a long, tile-topped cob wall.   Follow the track, now ungrassed, into an open area where there are two more gates to your left, the first of which leads onto a fenced track to Bagber Farm and the second leads into another field.   There is another large oak by the cob wall which is still on your right and two barns in the gated yard beyond.   Over on your left, there is a deep wood as you follow the steep, stony track with a grass verge past the entrance into the RH field which has a Bridleway arrow on its gatepost.   At the top of the track, two gates cross your route with two Bridleway arrows on the central gatepost.   Go through the RH of the two gates where the route to the right goes back to Gallows Corner.   You want the straight-on route which keeps to the LH hedge, past the cattle trough and with fine views beyond the open field on your right.

Follow the track along the edge of this long field and go through the small, arrow-signed gate in the old hawthorn hedge in the far LH corner.   This next track was overgrown with nettles when I came this way but, depending upon season and the farmer's workload, you may be more fortunate.   However, descending into a slight valley and up the other side, the next small gate in the facing hedge leads you into a very wide, dropping field with extensive views to the higher ridges which bound The Blackmore Vale - target of our Northbound leg on Day 3.   The arrows on the gatepost indicate two Bridleways.   You need to turn left and follow the LH, sparse hedge with the odd ash tree along the top of this field.   You now have views down into the valley to Dewlish, the final village before the end of your Day's walk at Tolpuddle.

At the end of this high field, check the direction of the Bridleway arrow on the post of the half-gate and go through into the next large field.   Begin to cross by aiming for the large barn which you will see far ahead of you in Dewlish but, when you get to the embankment which crosses the field from top to bottom, stop and look for the far LH end of the field where you will see an opening in the opposite hedge.   This is where you will be leaving the field so, if the layout of electric fences is different when you get here, that opening is you target.   You will see cattle troughs in the hedges either side of your path as you approach the gap which will soon show itself to be there for the main chalk track which is joining you from your top left.   On the track, go through the hedge, past a small wicket gate onto the banked field on your left and past a gate-sized opening into the field on your right.   Now, just follow the track downhill with grassy slopes on the left and with a scrub-filled gully in front of the old hedge down on your right.   As your track reaches an open area on the right, you will see the remains of cattle pens beyond the deep gully and a Bridleway arrow on a post pointing back the way have just come.

Keep straight on down your high hawthorn enclosed track with the slopes now wooded on the left and with another track reversing down on your right.   A signed Footpath descends off your track after the wire fence on your right but ignore it and keep following the chalky track.

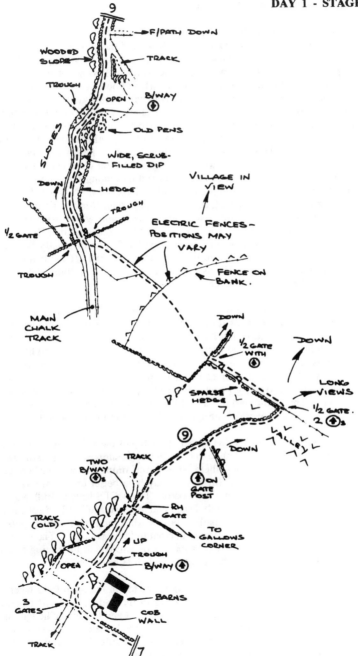

DAY 1 - STAGE 9

DEWLISH TO MILBORNE WOOD

This is a nice, steady stroll down into Dewlish with the wooded slopes still up on your left and the valley of the Devil's Brook beyond the houses which are built on its banks on your right.   The track soon becomes tarmac as you approach the village and, opposite a modern brick and flint house on the LH corner at the end of the lane, there is a pleasant, fence-enclosed grass area where you can sit on a strong bench for a few moments.   Beneath the willows, you will notice that the road bridge was constructed by the **DCC** in 1831.   The clear chalk stream which flows through this haven is Devil's Brook but the source of its name is more remote than the source of the stream which issues from the chalk ridge on the Southern edge of The Blackmore Vale at Ansty, only about 3 miles from Milton Abbas.   Dewlish is another of those Dorset villages which grew up along the edge of a vital clear chalk stream before it became possible to bring water to farms and cottages along pipes thus enabling farms to be built almost anywhere.   In the Domesday Book, *Devenis* was held by Earl Alan for the King but, long before that, this was an important Roman village.   When a tree was blown down in 1740, a huge section of black and white pavement was found measuring '65 paces by 15'.   The site was further excavated in 1790 when a tiled gutter of finest red brick clay was found all round it.   The originally Norman Chapel of All Saints is situated at the South end of Dewlish, just off the main road, but we won't be venturing there today as you've already come a long way and another diversion may be asking too much.

After a short rest, as you still have a couple of miles to go to today's journey's end, go back onto the lane and walk down to the T-junction where you turn left and go past a farm house and a track which leads to barns down on your right.   Now, steadily walking uphill, go past several corrugated asbestos sheds on your right, past the old stables opposite the brick house and, still with the wooded slopes on your left, keep plodding upwards.   Go past a track which drops down on your right and, just after the woods begin on the right, go past the arrow-signed Footpath which descends into these woods.   This is the start of Park Hill woods which are hanging woods growing on the edge of the hill overlooking Dewlish House and grounds in the valley below.

When the road turns round the LH corner at the top of the hill, there are two farm gates facing you.   Ignore them.   Although a Bridleway is supposed to go straight on from here in the direction you want, there isn't a confirming arrow anywhere and a cool stroll through the edge of Park Hill woods may be a better choice anyway.   So, turn right at the gate and half-gate into the woods.   This DOES have a Bridleway arrow and the wide path leads through a mainly beech and ash wood full of bird song and dappled shade - but mind the roots in the path.   Follow this long path until it gets narrower and then look out for a turning off into an open field on your left.   There is a Footpath yellow arrow on the gatepost.   Don't miss it or you'll end up having to come back because the straight on path only goes to Dewlish House.

Now, with an old hedge on your left, go up to the top of the open field where you will find more fine views and, after a short zig-zag in the hedge, you will reach the other side of the field with a hedge facing you.   Turn right and follow the hedge until, about 50 yards from the field corner, you will find a trestle stile with Footpath arrows on both sides next to an elderberry bush.   Go over the stile and follow the hedge down with a view of the scrub covered valley facing you.

26

DAY 1 - STAGE 9

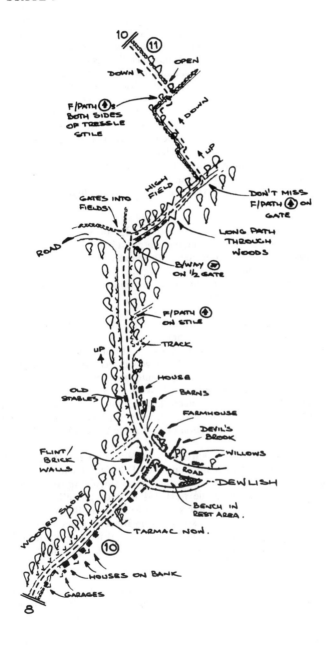

10

(11)

OPEN

DOWN

↓ DOWN

F/PATH ⊕s
BOTH SIDES
OF TRESSLE
STILE

↑ UP

HIGH
FIELD

DON'T MISS
F/PATH ⊕ ON
GATE

GATES INTO
FIELDS

ROAD

LONG PATH
THROUGH
WOODS

B/WAY ㊗
ON ½ GATE

F/PATH ⊕
ON STILE

TRACK

UP
↑

HOUSE

OLD
STABLES

BARNS

FARMHOUSE

DEVIL'S
BROOK

FLINT/
BRICK
WALLS

WILLOWS

ROAD

·DEWLISH

BENCH IN
REST AREA.

WOODED SLOPES

TARMAC NOW.

(10)

HOUSES ON BANK

GARAGES

8

DAY 1 - STAGE 10

MILBORNE WOOD TO 113 TRIANGULATION

In no time at all, you arrive in the valley bottom with a rough, hawthorn-bedecked patch ahead of you and with an opening into the field on your right.   Bear left and, past the end of the hedge on your left, join the wide, grassy Bridleway which comes down from behind the hedge.   Bearing right onto the track, 3 arrows on the gatepost show that the Bridleway runs along the main track whilst a Footpath turns off through the open gateway on your left.   Keep to the Bridleway and carry on up the track, between hedges, into Milborne Wood itself onto a narrow, tree-enclosed path with wild garlic in the early summer.   At a division of paths, signed with arrows on the dividing tree, the Footpath bears left whilst the Bridleway bears right.   Follow the Bridleway.   Milborne Woods' hazels have been heavily coppiced over the years and, after a stile into a field on your right, the hazels were coppiced to stumps on the left when I came by last.   Farming of these trees has allowed a huge variety of plants to survive and thrive in the clearings and, as you continue up the path, you will meet primroses, ramsons, bluebells, foxgloves, nettles or head-high thistles depending on the time of year.

Suddenly, you emerge into an open field with a hedge on your right but keep straight on, down and up, with the path submerged in a ditch alongside the hedge, until you come into a short, similar tunnel of trees with an oak at its entrance.   Now, take care! You leave the 'tunnel' through a gap alongside a half-gate but, being wary of overhanging branches and long nettles, you may find yourself on the A354 and being mown down by a passing juggernaut.

So, leave carefully and cross over to the other side.   Turn left and follow the road for 30 yards only before diving for cover into a wide, possibly overgrown, entrance to the signposted "Bridleway to Tolpuddle 1.1/4".   At last.   The end of Day 1 actually gets an official mention.   Go past another huge oak tree, with a hedge on the left and a short section of wire fence on the right, into another narrow path in a hollow. Instantly, there are high hedges either side with occasional oaks on the right and beeches on the left and you soon emerge into a lighter part of the path with sparse bushes on both sides.   Now, be warned.   There is supposed to be a Bridleway arrow pointing straight on up the continuation of your route but I didn't find one.

However, at an opening on your left which leads into a field, there IS a Bridleway arrow which points to the wide path along the LH hedge of said field.   This leads to Bladon Poultry Farm and Milborne St Andrew and is singular in its lack of interest to us, today.   However, I found the next 1/4 mile of tunnelled Bridleway to be completely overgrown and impassable so I had to go down the signed route as far as some old broken sheds where a track leads from Bladon Farm on the left and up the sloping field on the right.   I turned up this track until it came out into the top field and then turned right into this field until it led me back, through the trees at its far corner, onto the original Bridleway.

I share this diversion with you just in case Dorset Council haven't managed to have your path kept clear when you arrive.   All being well, you'll be able to keep straight on, though, until you leave the hedged-in Bridleway onto a wide grass track along the hedge on the left of the next field.   In a few upward yards, you pass the high spot of this down, at 113 m, and, at the end of this long field, you go through the Bridleway and Footpath-signed gate onto a descending track.

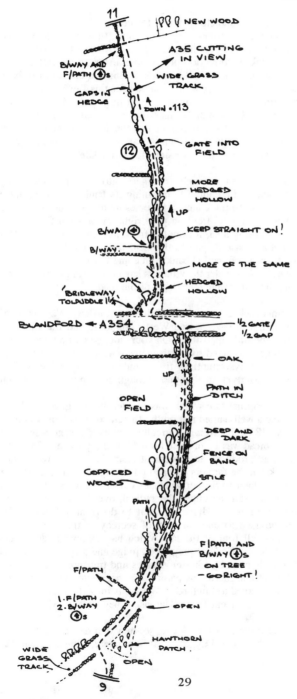

11

New Wood

A35 CUTTING IN VIEW

B/WAY AND F/PATH ④s

WIDE, GRASS TRACK

GAPS IN HEDGE

DOWN •113

⑫

GATE INTO FIELD

MORE HEDGED HOLLOW

UP

B/WAY ④

KEEP STRAIGHT ON!

B/WAY.

MORE OF THE SAME

OAK

HEDGED HOLLOW

'BRIDLEWAY TOLPUDDLE 1¼

BLANDFORD ← A354

½ GATE/ ½ GAP

OAK

UP

PATH IN DITCH

OPEN FIELD

DEEP AND DARK

FENCE ON BANK

COPPICED WOODS

STILE

PATH

F/PATH AND B/WAY ④s ON TREE — GO RIGHT!

F/PATH

1. F/PATH
2. B/WAY ④s

OPEN

WIDE GRASS TRACK

HAWTHORN PATCH.

OPEN

9

29

113 TRIANGULATION TO TOLPUDDLE

From the last gate, you can see Puddletown across the deep valley over on your right. This will be your first small town, tomorrow. For now, though, keep on down the grassy track alongside the LH hedge to the next gate in the facing hedge. Stand awhile at this gate and check the direction of the blue arrow on the left post. This points across the next, 1/4 mile wide, field towards the highest bushes in sight on the other side - as per the sketch. Changes are planned for this field because, on 31st January 1992, a Planning Notice was issued regarding the A35 Tolpuddle and Puddletown Northern By-pass for which villagers have been campaigning for years. For the purposes of this book, we have to assume that the delay will continue and that you won't find a By-pass across your path when you arrive. If it's here, carry out the time-honoured procedure and follow the diversions for Tolpuddle.

However, go through the signed, wrought-iron gate into a deep, hawthorn lined Bridleway with harts-tongue and common ferns lining its banks, and descend into a green, dappled wood. Follow the track until it becomes more open and joins a gravel track in an open area with a 'Private' field on your right and a gated field on the left corner. After a private parking area, follow the track past the rows of gardens and houses down on the right and past the gate to the Cemetery on the left. Around the bend in the track, with trees up on the LH bank, you come out onto the horribly busy A35. What a nightmare! No wonder the villagers have been campaigning for a By-pass to save them from the intolerable leviathans of the road.

A confirmation post points back up our route - "Bridleway to Dewlish". Turn left and keep to the pavement until you have passed West Farmhouse and the Church of St John the Evangelist over the wall opposite. On your side, go past a thatched cottage and a row of brick cottages protected by a raised pavement and a short section of railing. Here, look both ways countless times and dash across the A35 to the sanctuary of the Tolpuddle Martyrs' tree ground, through the gap in the wooden fence.

Past the offspring of the original tree which was planted by the great Trades Union stalwart, Len Murray, take a well-earned rest on the thatch-covered bench and I'll tell you a story. In the year 1833, the average agricultural worker's wage was 10/- (50p) per week and, as a guide, bread was 1/- or more for a 4lb loaf (5p for a 1.75 kilo loaf). The latest negotiations had produced an agreement from the farmers to award a pay increase to 10/- per week but the farmers reneged on the agreement and cut workers' wages to 9/- per week and later to 8/- per week.. Under the leadership of George Loveless, a Chapel man and thus an unpopular radical, over forty workers formed a legal Friendly Society, asking for advice on what to do from a Trade Society in London. They were advised to take an oath of secrecy in the dealings of their Friendly Society and thus fell foul of the law which had outlawed secret societies during the Napoleonic Wars. Under a prejudiced judge and jury, six of the leaders were found guilty of conspiracy at Dorchester Assizes and transported to America for life. However, all did not end there. A pardon was negotiated by interested M.Ps and, by 1838, all six had returned to England. What it is important to realise is that The Tolpuddle Martyrs did not invent Trades Unions. They already existed.

However, you've completed the first leg of your journey and deserve a rest. Come back here when you're ready to start Day 2. It'll be a lovely, quite different, Day.

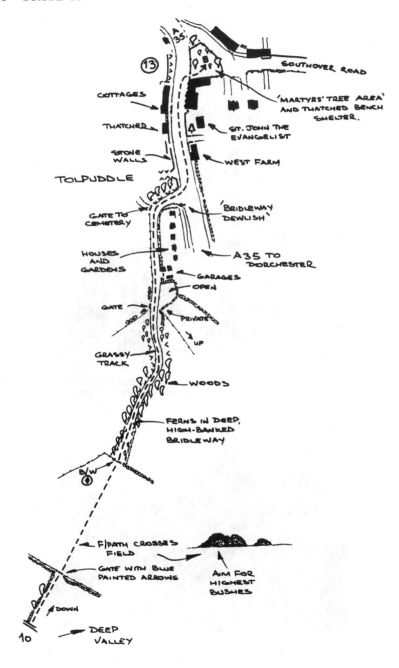

THE BLACKMORE VALE PATH

DAY 1 - STAGE 11

⑬

SOUTHOVER ROAD

COTTAGES

'MARTYRS' TREE AREA'
AND THATCHED BENCH
SHELTER.

THATCHED

ST. JOHN THE
EVANGELIST

STONE
WALLS

WEST FARM

TOLPUDDLE

GATE TO
CEMETERY

'BRIDLEWAY
DEWLISH'

HOUSES
AND
GARDENS

A35 TO
DORCHESTER

GARAGES

OPEN

GATE

PRIVATE

UP

GRASSY
TRACK

WOODS

FERNS IN DEEP,
HIGH-BANKED
BRIDLEWAY

B/W
④

F/PATH CROSSES
FIELD

GATE WITH BLUE
PAINTED ARROWS

AIM FOR
HIGHEST
BUSHES

DOWN

10

DEEP
VALLEY

31

TOP: STS. PETER AND PAUL, BLANDFORD FORUM - PAGE 10

BOTTOM: SOUTHOVER ROAD, TOLPUDDLE - PAGE 34

DAY 2 - INTRODUCTION

TOLPUDDLE TO DORCHESTER

There are far less hills to struggle up today and, as much of the journey is along the valleys of the Rivers Piddle and Frome, you would expect it to be perfectly flat. Let me tell you, it's not all flat because the A35 tends to follow the level ground, along the river terraces, and we don't want to follow the major trunk road from London to Cornwall all day, do we? This is unashamedly Thomas Hardy country and, although Dorset County Council has produced a Trail for motorists and our colonial friends from across the Atlantic, it's far better to keep away from the crowds and just appear - fleet of foot and suddenly out of nowhere - amongst his many admirers who we will meet occasionally. Every town and village which we see today dates back to at least the Domesday Book and farming continues just as it always has done, albeit more mechanised and employing far less farm labourers - a change which caused intense concern to Hardy as far back as the mid-1800s.

You start at the Tolpuddle Martyrs' memorial tree where you finished Day 1 and pass through ancient farmland and woods, both inhabited by strange sunken bowls of geological interest. The route visits several villages, so you need never starve or die of thirst, and you can linger at some fine churches and restful spots by tinkling chalk streams on your approach to the County town of Dorset. Here, within striking distance of the Durotrigian hill fort of Maiden Castle, the Romans built the walled city of Durnovaria - and here the shorter Day 2 ends with plenty of time to explore.

	STAGE	MILES	TOTAL MILES
1.	Tolpuddle to Park Farm	1.00	1.00
2.	Park Farm to Admiston	1.00	2.00
3.	Admiston to Puddletown	1.75	3.75
4.	Puddletown to Hardy's Cottage	1.25	5.00
5.	Hardy's Cottage to Lower Bockhampton	1.50	6.50
6.	Lower Bockhampton to Frome Meadows	1.00	7.50
7.	Frome Meadows to Dorchester	1.00	8.50

DAY 2 - STAGE 1

TOLPUDDLE TO PARK FARM

With all the talk about the Tolpuddle Martyrs, I didn't tell you anything else about Tolpuddle. So before you leave - Tolpuddle takes its name from *"Tola"*, wife of Orcus, founder of the Abbey at Abbotsbury and an officer under King Canute whilst, in the Domesday Book, 'the same church (Abbotsbury) holds *Pidele*'. "Park Pale" is an area a little below Athelhampton and this was probably a park of the abbot of Abbotsbury or the Martyns of Athelhampton. Our route goes through Park Farm in just a mile from here. The only other information which I managed to glean from Hutchin's 'History and Antiquities of Dorset' is that the church of St John the Evangelist was restored in 1855 and it was "a small and ancient fabric".

Now, leave the thatched shelter and head due South down Southover Road, not failing to admire the long thatch on the LH corner and the twin river arches under the old mill on your left as you cross the first bridge. Carry on along the lane, passing the 'Private' field on your right and the gunnera-lined wall on the left, until you have crossed two more stream bridges and arrived at a LH bend in the road. The bridges all span streams which link up just 1/4 mile downstream to become the River Piddle and thus reclaiming the name of the stream which earlier flowed down the Piddle Valley to Puddletown (3 miles from our start today). At the bend, go straight on, past the Bridleway post facing you and onto the track which leads to a couple of cottages. Turn right where the short hedge ends, through the small gate with a Bridleway arrow and, in this first field of the Day, follow the RH hedge and veer slightly left towards the far end. There you will find a farm gate which leads you out onto a tarmac track which joins you from your left.

On the other side of the track stand a derelict barn and what was once a fine farm house. There is a Bridleway arrow on the corner post of the wire fenced field on your left as you start on the long, rough farm track, past a cantilever gate across your path and with a wire fence followed by a grassy patch and a hedgerow on your right

Keep straight on, past a couple of huge oak trees, one either side, and a gate on your left which leads into a field in which lurks a tree and scrub-filled, deep, mysterious, bowl. These bowls are a phenomenon in this area and you will see several, all smaller than this one, as you progress today. They are swallow-holes or 'dolines', the largest of which is 'Cull-pepper's Dish', about 2 miles East from here and well known to geologists. Dolines are holes down which acidic surface waters soak away, dissolving the underlying chalk and causing the topsoil to sink into the ensuing hollow.

Carry on, with beech trees on your right and the stream visible in the meadow, until you arrive at a junction of gates with a signed Footpath on the left and a Bridleway sign on the gatepost facing you. Go through the gate onto the gravel drive for Park Farm, with planted willows and beeches either side of the drive. Quietly pass the house and the cotoneaster-covered wall of the adjacent barn. Pass the RH holly hedge and go through the next gate across your route into the gravel turning circle for the residents' cars. Past the house on your left, go through the left of the two wrought-iron gates, signed with a Bridleway arow, and cross the short field to a gate and stile in the tree-filled hedge. Over the stile, you are in a field which slopes up to your left with a hedge on your right

THE BLACKMORE VALE PATH

DAY 2 - STAGE 1

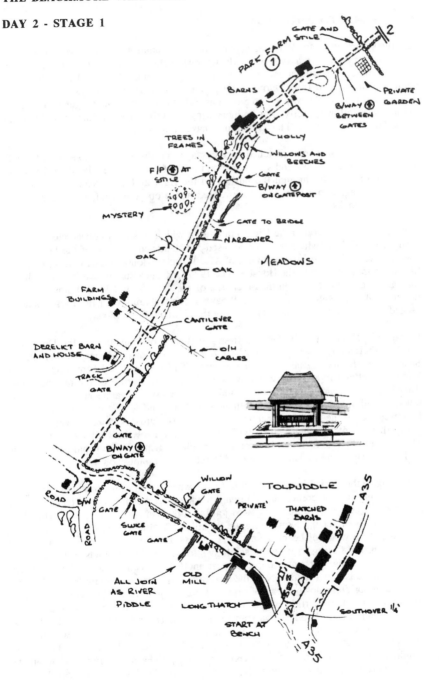

PARK FARM STILE
①

GATE AND STILE

2

BARNS

PRIVATE GARDEN

B/WAY BETWEEN GATES

TREES IN FRAMES

HOLLY

WILLOWS AND BEECHES

F/P ⊕ AT STILE

GATE

B/WAY ⊕ ON GATE POST

MYSTERY

GATE TO BRIDGE

NARROWER

OAK

MEADOWS

OAK

FARM BUILDINGS

CANTILEVER GATE

DERELICT BARN AND HOUSE

O/H CABLES

TRACK

GATE

GATE

B/WAY ⊕ ON GATE

ROAD

B/W

WILLOW GATE

TOLPUDDLE

A35

GATE

'PRIVATE'

THATCHED BARNS

ROAD

SLUICE GATE

GATE

ALL JOIN AS RIVER PIDDLE

OLD MILL

LONG THATCH

START AT BENCH

'SOUTHOVER ¼'

A35

DAY 2 - STAGE 2

PARK FARM TO ADMISTON

Past the sycamore on the RH hedge, you arrive at a small gate across your path. Go through onto a wide, grassy track with two farm gates either side (and not an arrow between them). Passing a grassy bank on the right, you are close to the route of the ancient Roman Road from Durnovaria (Dorchester) to Badbury Rings nr. Wimborne which continued all the way to Old Sarum nr. Salisbury. It is no longer visible here but it can be followed easily after Badbury Rings and the route is described clearly in Book Two of this series, "The Cranborne Chase Path".

However, keep going, past thatched Park Cottage and its cob walled shed on the left and several willows, oaks and sycamores on the right. At the left bend in the track, the stream is visible through the bushes on the right and, after you have passed a thatched cottage and a fine, old stone-roofed house on your right, you reach a wide junction of tracks.

The right turn takes you to the Victorian church which was only consecrated on New Year's Eve 1861 but which is no longer used. It stands on the edge of the lane which used to lead to the East Front entrance of Athelhampton House and was built to replace the old church adjacent to the House. The 1937 Ordnance Survey map No. 140 shows this lane and, in the hedge on the other side of the very busy A35 still stands one of the original stone gateposts - but you'll have to run the gauntlet of the juggernauts to go and see it - and this, presumably, is why the church fell out of use.

Listed under *Pidele*, held by Ohdold from the Bishop of Salisbury, in the Domesday Book, Athelhampton was *Aethelhelm's tun* the farmhouse of one Aethelhelm, a Saxon-English owner, one of the Saxon earls of Dorset who led forces against the Danes at Portland in 837 AD where he was killed. Almost all of the present house dates back to the earliest Tudor times and is well worth a separate visit. There are links through marriage between Athelhampton House and Kingston Lacy but, for our purposes today, the slight connection with Thomas Hardy is more relevant. It is likely that Hardy's father helped with the restoration of the Hall roof and young Thomas, himself a formidable architect, made a water colour painting of the buildings. But more of Thomas Hardy, Dorset's most famous son, later.

Returning to the tracks' junction, bear left from whence you came, past an opening to farm buildings on the corner, into an uphill track between dense hedged banks. After a gate on your right, you cross a field-joining alley via two small gates with blue-painted arrows on them. Now, continue, uphill, past bluebells if it's the right time of year, into a wood of beeches and oaks. Ignore all paths and openings and go straight on, not failing to note the small swallow-holes and mounds in the dappled shade of the woods. You now descend, past another LH path, to a Bridleway-signed gate which leads into a field. Note the direction of the arrow and aim for the LH end of the farm buildings down ahead of you. Find the gate in the low corner, passing barns and a pit on your right on the way, and emerge onto the concrete track which swings round to dairy buildings on your right. Turn left and go down the track, past two Bridleway arrows on the fence opposite the next gate on your left which leads onto another Bridleway bound for Southover Heath. The fine old, stone farmhouse standing beyond the barns on your right is Admiston Farm but keep on down the track, passing newly-planted trees, the private drive to the house on your right and a gate on your left.

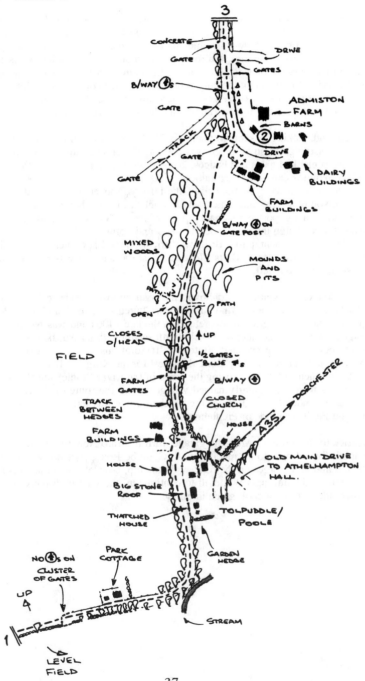

DAY 2 - STAGE 3

ADMISTON TO PUDDLETOWN

At the end of the concrete track, go through the wooden gates, past the gates on your right, and out onto the road.   I apologise for the next 3/4 mile but, due to the ancient origins of the network of by-ways and tracks, together with the meandering of the River Piddle and its tributaries, the route from Tolpuddle to Puddletown is nowhere near a straight line.   Come to think of it, the main A35 isn't at all straight either. What I'm trying to say is that the only way from here to Puddletown is along the road - and it has no pavements or verges.   There are no convenient paths so, for this section, you will have to exercise caution and hope for a safe deliverance.

Turn right and, tacking to keep yourself visible to oncoming traffic, follow the lane uphill.   Passing gates on your left and a Footpath-signed gate on your right which only leads to blocked gates and hedges, keep going up to a left bend at the top of the hill which requires care in its negotiation.   At least, after this bend, it's downhill all the way to Puddletown.   At the end of the lane, you meet the A35 with all its fury again - but you now have a pavement and it's only 100 yards before you leave it.   On the RH corner, a signpost points back up your lane to "Tincleton 1.3/4 miles" whilst, opposite, the road sign indicates "Dorchester 5 and Tolpuddle 1.3/4".   Turn left and follow the A35 pavement, past a Bridleway arrow on the LH corner gate which shows the route to Ilsington, across Butts Close and past the telephone box to a garage and petrol station on your left.

If you would like to explore Puddletown, the road opposite leads to Ilsington House and The Square where you will find Puddletown Church.   The Church of St Mary the Virgin is Norman in origin.   It was rebuilt in the late 1400s and was reconsecrated as long ago as 1505.   The interior is well worth seeing with its oak box-pews and fine roof - it seems to have escaped Victorian 'restorations'.   Domesday lists Puddletown as *Piretone*, held by Bolle the priest for the King.   It was later changed to Piddleton, then Piddletown (using the name of the River Piddle) but this was again changed - as were all similarly named villages along the route of the river - by the Victorians, to Puddletown.   Perhaps the Northern route was seldom travelled and they didn't find Piddletrenthide or Piddlehinton.

Now, back to the route.   After the garage, turn left into New Street and follow this lane uphill for 1/4 mile to its junction with Coombe Road, past houses and cottages on the left and high verges on the right.   At the top, bear left, with the Upper School now on your right, and pass Whitehill to continue up the lane with banks of beeches on either side offering a cool, green interlude.

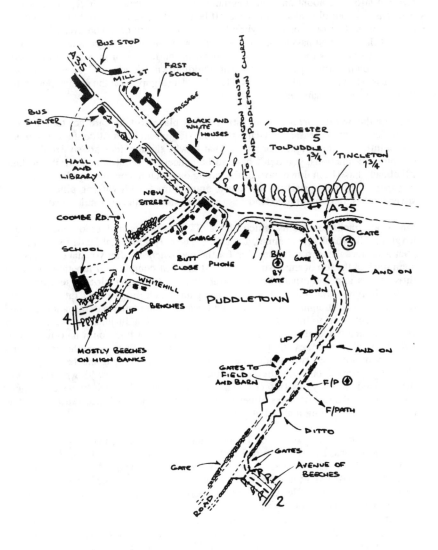

DAY 2 - STAGE 4

PUDDLETOWN TO HARDY'S COTTAGE

At the top of the hill, still between banked and shading trees, begin a downhill stroll into 1/2 mile of farmland, passing a signed Bridleway on the farm track to your left and another right track which leads to a Footpath-marked stile.   The woods over on your right are a wing of Puddletown Woods, through which you will have a most pleasant stroll for about an hour, beginning in a few minutes.   Keep on down the lane, passing four old oaks on the next left bend and a gate on the right which gives a clear view of the woods on the skyline.   After a few more oaks and sycamores at the sides of the lane, you pass a narrow wood on your right with a huge pine close to the road - if it's been spared - and, at the LH bend in the road, you go straight on, across the RH road, into a parking area for Puddletown Woods.   Note: "Forestry Commission. Please Leave Gateway Clear".   The signpost on the corner points to - 'Bridleway. Yellowham Hill 1'.

Through this wood, constant 'Harvesting' takes place so take care not to get lost if slight detours are necessary.   Getting lost is MY job and I must confess that this is not an infrequent experience for me.   That is why these guides are so detailed.   At complicated junctions, you don't have to be concerned about which turning to take. I'll already have been down most of the wrong ones before consigning the right ones to paper.   Anyway, start up the sandy, gravely track with varying pines, beeches silver birches, oaks and rhododendrons on either side for the next mile or so.

Ignore all tracks and paths which shoot off at tangents and enjoy the fern and foxglove-filled banks (in summer, at least).   The only additional guide I shall give is 'belt and braces' security information for the *two junctions* after you have crossed the main track at the top of this rising path.   At the *first* complicated junction, there are three tracks and a footpath besides your own.   Counting clockwise from your approach, ignore the 1st track and the footpath which drops down into the forest. Keep on, almost straight, down the second track.   Later, after passing another track which branches off to the left, you will reach the *second* multi-junction.   Here, from your approach track, again counting clockwise, there is a track on a hairpin on your left and another track next to that.   Nearly opposite you, there is another track which instantly divides into two, whilst the last track is on your right and heads upwards. Go straight across, onto the dividing track and take the left fork, downwards.   Got that? Good. A few yards further down, take the right fork in the tracks and, after a couple of small swallow-holes either side of the track, you will see Hardy's Cottage through the trees straight ahead of you.

Even if you haven't read any of Thomas Hardy's wonderful, evocative stories and rather sad poems, I'm sure you will have seen the films of "Far from the Madding Crowds" or Polanski's version of "Tess" (of the D'Urbervilles).   Hardy was born here on 2nd June 1840 and his early years were spent in training and working as a very successful architect.   He began writing poetry whilst working in London between 1862 and 1867 and then he came back to live in Dorset and to assist John Hicks, his first employer, with a church restoration project.   A similar project in 1870, in St Juliot in Cornwall, introduced Hardy to Emma Gifford with whom he fell in love. Although he had finished his first draft novel by 1868, his first success was Desperate Remedies which was published in 1871, followed by Under the Greenwood Tree in 1872, A Pair of Blue Eyes in 1873 and Far From the Madding Crowd in 1874.   The rewards from these novels enabled Hardy to marry his Emma in 1874.

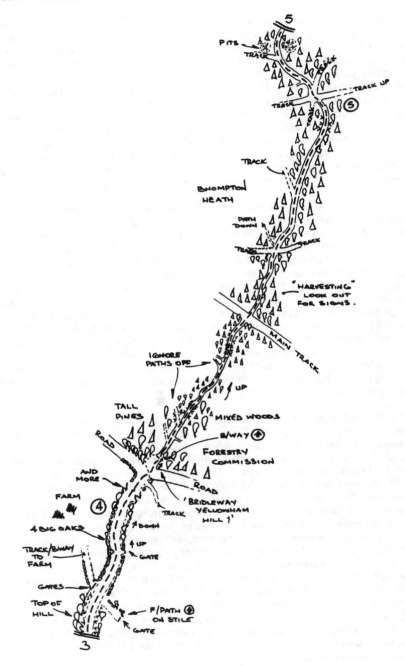

DAY 2 - STAGE 5

HARDY'S COTTAGE TO LOWER BOCKHAMPTON

We shall hear more about Thomas Hardy as our route leads us to several towns and villages which played a part in his life and work. For now, though, through the barrier which crosses the track, you emerge into a turning circle where a stone memorial recalls Hardy's work at this cottage and you can visit his garden through the gate a few yards down the signposted Higher Bockhampton path from whence come today's 'madding crowds'. Returning here, go up the steep, peaty Footpath which is signed for "Lower Bockhampton 1.1/2" and, where a path forks off right around the top end of Hardy's garden, keep left, past a Footpath arrow post next to a large beech. You are now right on the edge of Puddletown Forest and the ridge which crosses your path and follows it on your right, alongside the path, is a forest boundary line. Hardy's Cottage was outside the forest and you have now crossed back into it. Pass another Footpath marker post and continue to a couple of stiles and a gate in the right corner with Rushy Pond beyond the bushes near the top.

The Roman Road from Durnovaria to Londinium crosses our path down here but its route would be clearer by night as a Roman Centurion's ghost is said to walk it then. Don't follow the arrowed Footpath over the left stile to Norris Mill. Go over the un-arrowed, but pointer-indicated, stile next to the gate for 'Lower Bockhampton 1'. Follow the tree-lined path to a clearing where the path goes straight ahead and a low signpost points back up your arrival path to "Thorncombe Wood Trail". Don't follow the clearer path. Turn left down the less obvious path to a Footpath-signed gate and enter a long, wide field with a hedge on your right. This is commonly used for grazing cattle - a large variety - the white ones of which look like Charolais to me, but I'm no expert. A temporary electric fence runs parallel to the hedge to keep you and the cattle apart. After a set of gates which cross your path, you will find yourself leaving the field down a farm track with a permanent wire fence on your left and the hedge still on your right. After turnings into Pine Lodge Farm house and buildings on the right, a new line of sycamores leads you to the grass verged, stump protected exit with a LH corner gate.

Cross the road from Tincleton to Stinsford onto the opposite, stony track which is a signed Footpath for "Bhompston Farm". In Hutchins', *Bomston was formerly a manor and hamlet but is now (1861) only a farmhouse and some cottages'*. It still is. To get there, keep on along the track, passing a pair of gates in the hedge on your left and with an open field on your right. After a cottage on your left, the track bends left to Bhompston Farm and Norris Mill but our route follows the yellow arrowed and signposted path for 'Lower Bockhampton 1/4' which goes through the RH gate before "The Farmhouse". Past the garden, go through the next signed gate and follow the arrow's direction towards the stile in the far right corner, where the hedge joins the fenced row of trees. Over this stile, with an embankment running towards the approaching River Frome ahead on your left, veer slightly right, uphill, towards the LH end of the first red clay-tiled roof of the farm. There, you will find a Footpath-signed post next to the gate which leads you into the farm, across a short field, through another signed gate and into the farmyard with stables on your left and barns on your right. Keep on, through the last gate and quietly pass the lovely gardens and fine brick farmhouse on your right, joining the track which passes the gardens of cottages lining the road through Lower Bockhampton. Emerging onto the road, turn left, with the cob Bridge Cottage on the LH corner, and head down towards the river bridge.

THE BLACKMORE VALE PATH

DAY 2 - STAGE 5

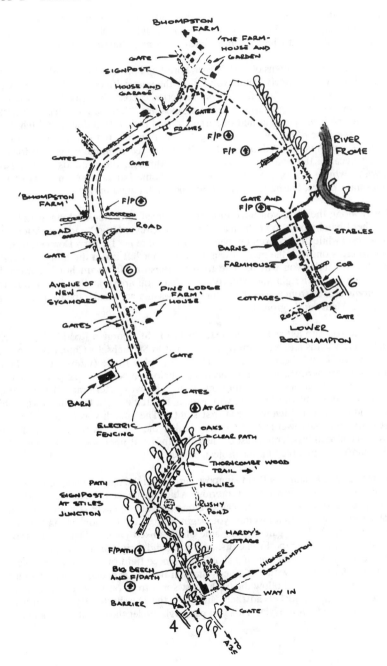

LOWER BOCKHAMPTON TO FROME MEADOWS

Before proceeding further, it may be worth mentioning that, up the road through Lower Bockhampton, on the left by the post box, stands the Old School House which was built in 1847 and at which Thomas Hardy was one of the first pupils.

Now, after the ups and downs of Puddletown Forest and the trail from Hardy's Cottage, this next Stage is completely flat as you follow the young River Frome and cross the meadows which grew lush and fertile from its periodic, controlled flooding. Arriving at the narrow Frome bridge, turn off at the signpost for "Stinsford 1/2 and Dorchester 1.1/4" onto the long, pleasant and tree-lined, raised path with a drainage ditch down on your left and the river down on your right. Within the first few yards the stream alongside the path is only a drainage stream which is fed from the water meadows on your left because the real river takes a sweep through the grounds of Kingston Maurward, which was originally a fine stately home but is now an equally fine Agricultural College, before re-emerging just before the road bridge.

Half-way along the path, you have to cross a bridged farm track, along which 'the lowing herd wind slowly o'er the lea' (Thanks to Grey's Elegy) and, just after that, you can rest awhile on a convenient bench. But you're not far from Dorchester, now, so best to press on, with the main stream now on your left and a ditch on your right. In another 1/4 mile, you will be able to see Kingston Maurward house across the stream/ditch on your right and, shortly after that, you arrive at the spot where the River Frome arrives from across the water meadows and goes under the path on its way to Kingston Maurward's grounds.

Here, before you turn left at the signposted path to "St George's Road 3/4", you can go on for a few yards and then turn right for a visit to St Michael's Church at Stinsford where Thomas Hardy's heart is buried. He used to play fiddle (violin) in the church band for services at Stinsford and his heart truly belonged here. If the powers that be wanted to bury his ashes in Westminster Abbey, he was determined that his heart would remain in his beloved Dorset, with Emma, his first wife, at the church where his mother and father had fallen in love at first sight. The church was built in the early 13th Century and the tower is 14th Century whilst the Victorian restoration of 1868 seems to have been less 'enthusiastic' than that inflicted upon some other churches. Maybe Hardy was involved in this project, as well.

Returning to the St George's Road signpost, turn down the narrow path, reinforced on the river's edge, and follow it to a footbridge which spans the tributary along the edge of this open meadow which we met earlier along the path. There is a pleasant sound of water rushing over a small weir as you begin to cross the meadow, along the line of a series of extinct sluice-gates by the side of the raised path. Dorchester appears over on your right after the Frome disappears around a right bend and you continue across the meadow. At the end of a short, wire-fenced field on your left, go over the stile onto a chalky track with cattle pens through the LH gate and rough scrub along both sides of the track. Follow the track, past some trees on your left with a raised bank going up the field behind them and with the Dorchester By-pass embanked beyond paddocks on your right, until you pass right under the elevated, concrete road bridge.

THE BLACKMORE VALE PATH

DAY 2 - STAGE 6

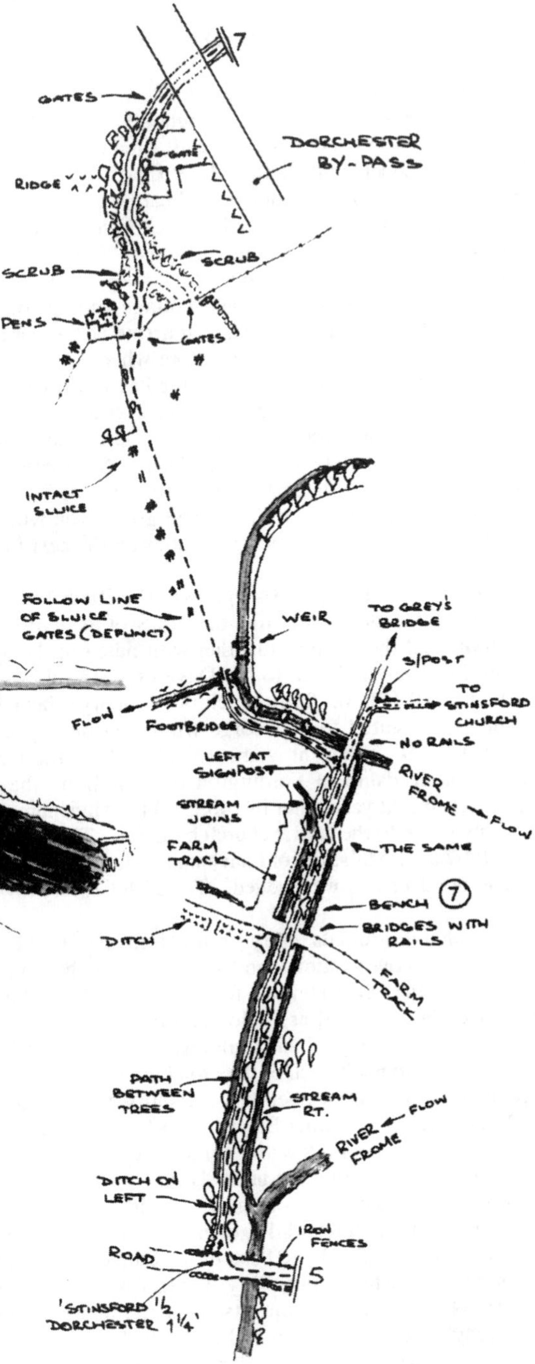

GATES

RIDGE

SCRUB

SCRUB

PENS

GATES

INTACT SLUICE

DORCHESTER BY-PASS

FOLLOW LINE OF SLUICE GATES (DEFUNCT)

WEIR

TO GREY'S BRIDGE

S/POST

TO STINSFORD CHURCH

NO RAILS

FLOW

FOOTBRIDGE

LEFT AT SIGNPOST

STREAM JOINS

FARM TRACK

RIVER FROME ← FLOW

R THE SAME

BENCH ⑦

BRIDGES WITH RAILS

DITCH

FARM TRACK

PATH BETWEEN TREES

STREAM RT.

RIVER ← FLOW FROME

DITCH ON LEFT

ROAD

IRON FENCES

5

'STINSFORD 1½ DORCHESTER 1¼'

DAY 2 - STAGE 7

FROME MEADOWS TO DORCHESTER

Beyond the fly-over, follow the track round to the left and over the major River Frome bridge, with a farm track continuing straight on. Go past the farm track on your right and the turn to your left and, passing a wide area in which a couple of cars may park, you arrive at a paddock on the left. After the paddock, you are in St George's Road and you turn right here at the stone-walled barn on the corner for the final, easy walk into Dorchester - not missing the 'village' of Fordington on the way. Stay on the RH pavement along here, past the thatched "Riverkeeper's Cottage" and a few remaining farm buildings on your side of the road. There are more modern houses on the other side and an older, thatched cottage (no.20) on the corner of Ackerman Street. Then, after a telephone box, you arrive at the corner of the A352 Wareham road which is graced by a convenient store where you can buy reviving drinks and snacks. Still keep on the RH side of the road as you reach the five-ways junction and, with a newsagents shop behind you, cross over Kings Road into High Street, Fordington by using the pedestrian refuge. Here is another 'phone box so you can call for a return lift home if you need one later. Now, carry on up the hill, past or via the Bull's Head and past the RH turnings for Hillside Terrace (pedestrians only) and Church Acre. When you reach the village green, you will find a couple of benches under the trees with the Post Office and Stores on the next LH corner.

"Fordington" denotes a ford or passage over the River Frome where there is now the A35 road bridge 1/4 mile North from the corner of St George's Road. Domesday lists it as *Fortitone* and these lands, together with much of the area around and including Dorchester, has been assigned to the Duke of Cornwall since the 16th year of the reign of Edward III (1343). The church of St George, behind the iron railings up on your right, is dedicated to St George whose earlier appearance, at the Battle of Dorylaeum in 1097, when he same to the aid of the Crusading William Belet, recipient of the lordship of Fordington from William the Conqueror, ensured this dedication, albeit 300 years later in 1405. The tympanum over the inside porch door was probably given to the earlier church by Belet. The whole church was extensively rebuilt in 1907 and, whilst the old nave and aisle were extended, a new North arcade, chancel and South chapel were added. The 15th Century tower remains, thankfully.

Leaving the church grounds, carry on up High Street and, just before Pound Lane, notice the lovely bow-windows on two storeys of the house opposite. Downhill, the pavement on the left is elevated for a while, with handrails, as it runs past a long row of terraced houses. After Holloway Road goes back on your right, High Street keeps on going, past the yard and buildings of a former mill on the right which used to draw its power from a branch of the Frome on its far side. You have now arrived in the wide junction of High Street and Salisbury Street (on the left) with High East Street, Dorchester. The former Baptist chapel facing you is now the Kingdom Hall of Jehovah's Witnesses. Follow the corner round to the right and you will find the River Frome's tributary flowing under High East Street and running under a timber extension from the back of the old mill. A little further down, past another 'phone box, is the Exhibition Hotel whilst, over the road stands the White Hart, next to the issuing River Frome. On the RH end of the bridge wall, you will find the entrance to the riverside walk which starts Day 3 but, for now, feel free to go and explore Dorchester, its churches, its shops, its cafes and pubs and, of course, to go and visit Thomas Hardy's statue at the top end of High West Street - passing William Barnes outside St Peter's on the way. We'll meet up here when you are ready for Day 3.

THE BLACKMORE VALE PATH

DAY 2 - STAGE 7

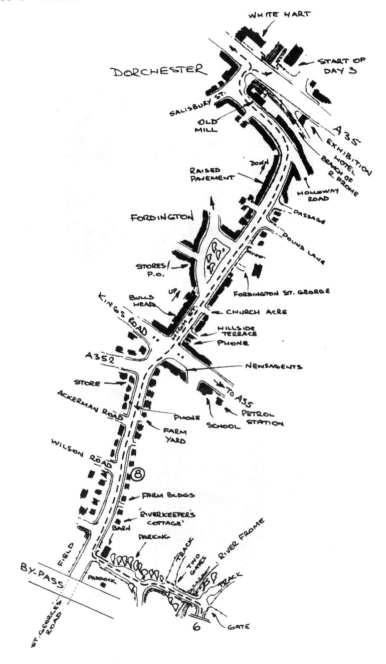

THE BLACKMORE VALE PATH

TOP: FROME WHITFIELD PATH, DORCHESTER - PAGE 50

BOTTOM: PITCHMARKET, CERNE ABBAS - PAGE 62

DAY 3 - INTRODUCTION

DORCHESTER TO MINTERNE MAGNA

Having spent some time exploring Dorchester, you will probably have found the statues commemorating the lives of Thomas Hardy and William Barnes, the first being Dorset's most famous author and poet whilst Barnes, the more optimistic of the two, produced many wonderful poems concerned with everyday life in rural Dorset. Sadly, Barnes has remained largely unappreciated outside this County because he was determined to maintain the language of his youth and his poems are nearly all written in the Dorset dialect.   However, after a few minutes reading, the code is not too difficult to break and the warmth, humour and wry observations of this gentle man's works are laid out for all to savour.   There'll be more about Barnes when we come to the towns and villages associated with him later on our travels.

Today, whilst walking through typical West Dorset countryside, you will notice that most of the land is given over to cereal production.   The flinty, chalky soil is ideal for corn, wheat and, over the past few years, oil seed rape for cattle feedstuffs.   The hordes of sheep have been replaced by acres of waving corn but, here and there, you will still meet a few cattle and sheep, mostly in the lowlands.   You will be moving generally Northwards to the edge of William Barnes' Blackmwore Vale (No, that's not a misprint - that's a sample of Dorset dialect) where yellowhammers and skylarks, together with the high-flying buzzards, will announce your approach into the warm and beautiful Cerne Valley villages of Godmanstone, Nether Cerne, Cerne Abbas and Journey's end at Minterne Magna.   You'll find the landscape changing quite clearly as you progress from the river valleys towards the Blackmore Vale.   Enjoy the Day.

	STAGE	MILES	TOTAL MILES
1.	Dorchester to Higher Burton Farm	1.50	1.50
2.	Higher Burton Farm to Wolfeton Clump	2.00	3.50
3.	Wolfeton Clump to Forston Down	1.50	5.00
4.	Forston Down to Godmanstone	1.00	6.00
5.	Godmanstone to Pound Farm	1.00	7.00
6.	Pound Farm to Cerne Abbas	1.25	8.25
7.	Cerne Abbas to Giant Hill	0.75	9.00
8.	Giant Hill to Little Minterne Hill	1.75	10.75
9	Little Minterne Hill to Minterne Magna	0.75	11.50

One more thing, before you go.   Take a laurel leaf with you - preferably a fresh one so that it will still bend when you arrive in Cerne Abbas.   All will be revealed when you get there but it could be to your advantage.

DAY 3 - STAGE 1

DORCHESTER TO HIGHER BURTON FARM

If you are starting out today without having explored Dorset's County town, I hope you will come back and spend a day here. Make it a Wednesday and you'll catch the market as well. Hutchins clearly appreciated Dorchester, the Roman Durnovaria, as he eulogised about it as "this town, the capital of the county, where the assizes are held and the knights of the shire elected, is one of the neatest and most agreeable in the county, and exceeded by few in England". Dorchester is in the Domesday Book as *Dorecestre*: King's land with Brictward the priest holding the church. Its fine old buildings and its tree-lined walks are indeed 'most agreeable' and you really should visit the museum for a deeper appreciation of Dorset's history and landscape.

Now, lecture over, return to the White Hart which stands opposite the High Street from Fordington where you arrived on Day 2. Where it says "London Road", on the iron railings beyond the bridge, turn left through the barriers and onto the path which runs alongside the River Frome's tributary. Past footbridges over the river and hedges, allotments and benches on your right, you will see the rows of houses bordering inner Dorchester in Frome Terrace opposite. After the tree-topped bank above the red-brick retaining wall, you arrive at a junction of paths with a sluice-gate at the pool on your right and with the paths over the iron-railed bridge on your left going to Top O' Town House and The Walks (Both of which should be on your itinerary for your return visit to Dorchester). Turn right, past the pool and onto a narrower path between the ditch on your left and a wire-fenced field on your right. The river has left for a while but it'll be back through another sluice-gate in a minute.

Follow the path, past a large willow and some sycamores on the field edge, to a steel and concrete footbridge across the main flow of the three joining river branches and a small stream. I sheltered under this bridge in a sudden downpour but it's too low to stand up underneath it. Now, follow the wider track on the other side, between fenced park land with new frame-protected trees on either side at first Then, after a footbridge over a ford, the track bears left with a fenced wood on the left and more park land on the right. This is the ancient estate of Frome Whitfield which is listed in the Domesday Book as *Frome*, held by the (un-named) wife of Hugh FitzGrip and it supported 250 sheep and 1 ass. The Whitfields were bygone lords of the manor and the estate once supported three farms and its own church, St Nicholas', but it was already decaying by 1549 and the last rector listed was Henry James in Dec. 1584.

At the T-junction of tracks, the facing track is "Private Drive. To Farm Only" so, with the gated entrance into the woods on your left, turn right where the Footpath arrow on the RH corner tree directs up the main track, between wire fences and with frame-protected young trees on the left. After "Yalbury Park" house on your right, cross the road onto the unsigned Bridleway opposite with a tile-hung cottage on the RH corner. Go up the grassy track, past the driveway into Yalbury House and follow the hawthorn, elderberry and beech-hedged track gently upwards until you arrive at a large oak on the left, opposite a pair of farm gates. The path becomes decidedly narrower for the next 200 yards with a right-angled left bend on the way. At its end, the track turns sharp right again onto a wider grass track with another farm gate on your left. Follow the wide track, with masses of bracken in the hedges on either side, to join the wide, gravel track which comes from Higher Burton Farm on the left. Keep straight on up the track with a hedged field on your left and a wooden fence in the hedge on your right.

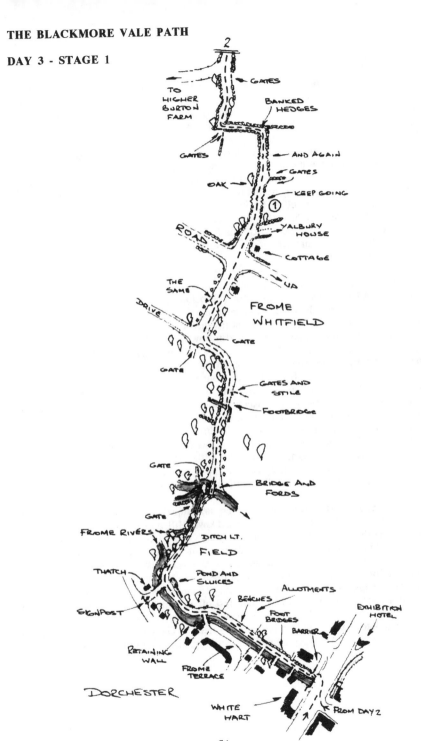

HIGHER BURTON FARM TO WOLFETON CLUMP

Just past an oak on the left, a track goes off into the field on your right. Keep straight on though, without any Bridleway signs, onto a very wide, hedge-lined, grassy ride which seems to be wide enough for an ancient two-carriage road. Follow the track up, past a small RH oak, elderberries and a small LH holly to the top where there is an opening into the field on your right as you plunge into a short, grassy alley. There is a good view of the hill-encompassed fields ahead from here before you begin to descend, round to the left of the hawthorn and beech clump which faces you, and follow the edge of the field to the bottom RH corner. There may be an electric fence lining the track around the field if sheep are being grazed here. Now, with a gate in the corner, follow the hedge round to the left. The hedge soon gives way to a wire fence with the valley side going up on your right and with a sheep pen on the right as well. At the end of this field, with two gates on the RH corner and two gates facing you, turn right onto the flinty track along the valley bottom from Higher Burton Farm.

Follow the track for about 200 yards until it turns right with a wide grassy area on your left. A field goes uphill ahead of you behind a solitary tree and a fuel storage tank. Turn left, onto the wide, grassy area and, before this direction leads you onto a narrow path between hedges, turn right (as directed by the Bridleway arrow on the wire-fence post) onto a cleared track and follow the LH hedge of the uphill field for 1/4 mile (It's a big field). If it helps, you should be heading due North. Anyway, in the top LH corner of the field, keep straight on, still on cleared track, with trees and bushes on your right and a low valley on your left. A similar track comes up from between two woods over on your left and both tracks merge at a sleeper-mounted Bridleway arrow on your right. Keep following the grassy track alongside the RH hedge, with a bigger wood in the left of the valley ahead of you, uphill for about 200 yards. At the top, a grass track goes off alongside a hedge on your left where you keep straight on past another Bridleway arrow on a vertical railway sleeper. You now begin a 150 yards slight descent - still with a RH hedge and a LH slope down to Wolfeton Clump woods - but, by a stile and a pair of gates in the fence, you are already engaged on another uphill trek of about 300 yards.

If you turn round and look behind you, there is a superb vista towards Dorchester and beyond to Hardy's monument on Black Down Hill above Portesham. No, not Thomas Hardy again. This high, stone tower, visible from all over South and West Dorset, commemorates Admiral Hardy, Nelson's flag captain at the Battle of Trafalgar. Now, turn back and, at the end of the fence as the track bends slightly left, look out for an indistinct path which plunges into a group of trees on your right. The track keeps on going so it would be easy to miss this turn. It IS signed with a Bridleway arrow but it's fixed to a tree just off the track. Also, it may be a bit overgrown. The path through these trees is only short, though, and you soon arrive at a small gate which leads you into a rising field. There are three Bridleway arrows on the gatepost but you keep straight on, anyway, keeping to the LH hedge to the top of the field.

THE BLACKMORE VALE PATH

DAY 3 - STAGE 2

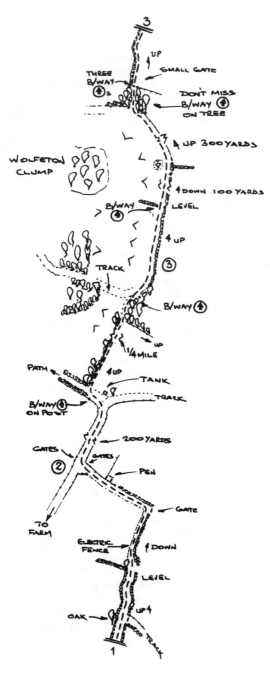

DAY 3 - STAGE 3

WOLFETON CLUMP TO FORSTON DOWN

At the top of the field, go over the stile in the wire fence.   As this is a Bridleway, I assume that horses can climb stiles.   Anyway, I've told Dorset County Council about it - and the overgrown woods at the beginning of this field - and the barb-wired gate and overgrown track ahead of you.   That surprised you, didn't it?   But I'm sure it will all have been cleared by the time this book is published.   Over the stile (or gate), follow the LH hedge and fence to the other end of the field where you will find two gates.   The gate on the right leads onto a private track down to Little Piddle Farm but the LH one leads onto a Bridleway which follows the RH, embankment-mounted hedge and fence through the next field.   Bridleway arrows are fixed to the gatepost - one either side - so I'm not leading you astray.   Follow the RH hedge to the end of this field and go through the Bridleway-arrowed gate into another field with a sparse hedge and a wire fence on your right, over which you can see down to Little Piddle Farm.   Go through the gate onto a wide track which runs down to the farm and cross the track to another gate in the facing hedge.   Go through the gate onto the road outside where you will find a Bridleway arrow on a low post.

Carefully cross the road and go through the farm gate or its adjacent 1/2 gate into the grassy patch opposite which houses an iron shed.   From this grassy patch, a path goes straight into the woods beyond.   This is the old path which is shown on the 1937 Ordnance Survey map but the current path keeps to the left of the woods so go round to the left past the shed and, when you get to a wire fence across your way, turn right alongside it for a few yards until you find a stile.   The trees are almost touching the fence but I'm sure you'll find the stile alright.   Climb over the stile (This is still Bridleway, by the way) and aim for the first electric pole on the right, from the edge of the woods.   Walk down the field, still aiming for the pole and, after a quick detour around or a plunge through a shallow swallow hole, you will arrive at a gate in the bottom LH corner of the field with a wire fence meeting the LH hedge.   There are fine views from this field, across to Charminster Down and to Hardy's monument, whilst the top of the chimney which appears above the near field skyline on your left belongs to Herrison Hospital, late departed casualty of the NHS cut-backs - I mean 'rationalisation'.

Through the gate, cross the road very carefully to the Footpath-arrowed gap in the hedge opposite.   On this side of the road, the farmer has supplemented the usual arrows with signs of his own which indicate which are Bridleways, which are Footpaths and which are Private routes across his land.   Very helpful indeed and much appreciated.   So, after the gap, head on down the field to the facing corner of the hedge and then follow the hedge down, past a cattle trough, to the bottom end of the field where a home-made sign indicates the direction of the Footpath straight across the farm track to Forston Higher Farm.   There is a small, fenced area on the left planted with copper-beeches and with another sign around the other side showing that the track is a Bridleway.   Cross over the track and head up the opposite field, past yet another sign against the RH hedge.   Forston is in the Domesday Book as *Foffardeston*, a former manor or hamlet, long since gone.   It was the seat of the Brownes of Frampton and the present house, rebuilt by Robert Browne, passed to his son John who "gave the mansion-house and appurtenances to be employed as a lunatic asylum for the county" - Hutchins.   This was the aforementioned Herrison Hospital.

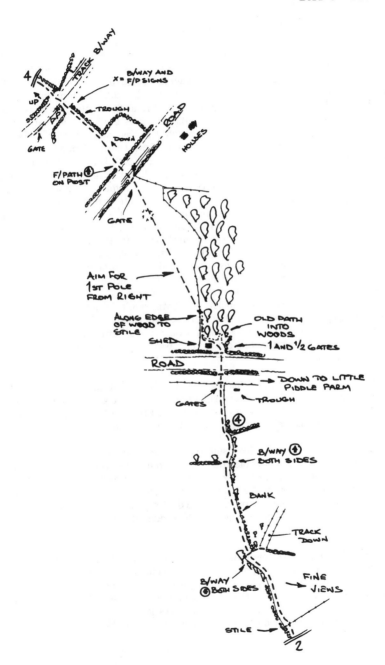

DAY 3 - STAGE 4

FORSTON DOWN TO GODMANSTONE

Follow the wide, cut Footpath around the edge of the field, uphill and, after a gap in the hedge, you arrive at the top of Forston Down and a gap in the RH hedge. The cut path clearly turns round to the left but this is signed "Private. No Access". You have to go through the RH gap and then follow the LH hedge steeply down to the valley where, after a cattle trough, you go back through the hedge to find a narrow gap cut in the next hedge facing you. This gap leads you into the valley bottom and a clearly cut path rises through the crops or grass up to the hedge at the top of the field opposite. Another gap is located exactly in the middle of the honeysuckled hedge at the top and you have to push your way through it to find painted yellow Footpath arrows on a post on the other side. Stop and take a bearing before you proceed across this heavy flint-strewn, high field and - 1: If the path is cut, follow it. 2: If the field is clear, aim slightly to the right of the swallow-hole in front of you, up and over the top and past the intruding hedge corner on your right. You will then see a track coming from the field on your right. Join it and follow it straight down to the far corner where it leaves your field, heading downwards. OR 3: If the field is planted and the path isn't clear, go round to the right side of the field, past the opening into the next RH field and up and over to join the track on the far RH side which leads to a descending exit from this field. This track is all flints and, after leaving the field, it turns an arc round to the right and goes uphill again between hedges. Don't follow it. Turn off to the left and follow the track along the LH hedge with the banked field on your right. There are clear views down into the Cerne River valley below you as the track bears off to a gate on your left. Again, don't follow it. Instead, go through the gate in the wire fence which crosses your path. There is a Bridleway arrow on the other side of the RH post and a painted yellow arrow on your side of the LH post. Follow the comfortable, grassy track which is cut into the steeply sloping East side of Cowdon Hill.

Looking ahead, you will notice that the Cerne Valley has a gentle slope on its left flank whilst the right flank is a great chalk escarpment. A good geologist will tell you why - probably something to do with speed and flow of ancient predecessors of the River Cerne and the erosion-resistance of different rocks.

After the track passes through a low-banked gully, go over the unmarked stile in the LH fence and walk down, under electric wires, to the track which runs through the bottom gate in the RH hedge and fence. There is an overgrown stile to the left of the gate. Turn right and follow the River Cerne which now runs parallel to the track which doubles as an official, although unsigned, Footpath. In a few moments, you will be able to see "The Smith's Arms", Godmanstone through a gap in the trees on the other side of the river.

Godmanstone is one of the few villages on our route which doesn't appear in the Domesday Book and the derivation of its name is uncertain. Hutchins conjectures that it is probably ecclesiastic from 'God-man's ton or Godwin's ton' Whatever, one of its earliest lords was Richard de Godmaneston who owned the lands with Mabel his wife in 1202. The little church is Norman in origin but it was much renovated in 1848 by a Mr Goodenough who rebuilt the chancel. It has three 17th Century bells in the tower.

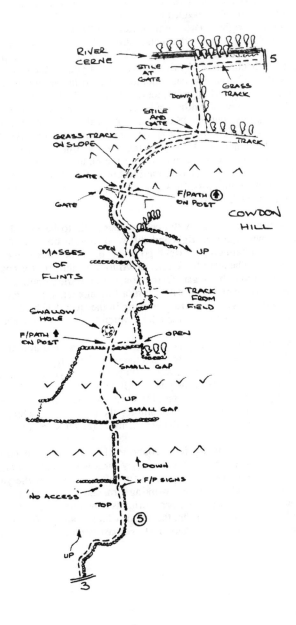

DAY 3 - STAGE 5

GODMANSTONE TO POUND FARM

As you follow the grassy track, the Cerne valley beckons and you are accompanied by the sound of the flint-bedded river on your left and by the steep slopes of Cowdon Hill over on your right.   Past the footbridge to "The Smith's Arms" - or back from "The Smith's Arms" - enjoy this gentle stroll along the riverside.   There is a river-cut ridge in the field opposite and a gate in the hedge across your path from where you can see the little church of Nether Cerne ahead of you.   Keep straight on, past a "Dogs on Leads Please" sign and past another little bridge across the river.   After this, at a wider, slower stretch of river, an oak tree stands defiantly in the river bed and, after another gate, a plank bridge leads across the river into a low field.   There are still no Footpath arrows but this IS official.   After the next gate, there is another gate facing you across the track as it zig-zags to go around the churchyard area.   Two side paths then lead through the LH hedge to the mainly flint-built Church of All Saints..   The tower is of flint and stone and, within the church, there is a 'probably' Norman font of Purbeck marble (not true marble but a fossil-packed limestone which can be polished to a high gloss. It was good enough for Salisbury Cathedral, so why not for this little church as well?).

Follow the track round, with trees on your right, to be joined by another track which comes down from your right and still keep straight on.   Past a tiled shed on the LH corner and a barn on your right, go across the wide track to the gate in the trees on the other side.   The main track runs down to your left, past a house behind a low stone wall.   Go through the gate facing you, with a warning notice concerning the privacy of some lakes which you will see in a few moments, and you will find yourself in a dark path with sycamore trees growing in the steep RH bank.   The LH trees border a garden at first, then they hide a lake which lies below the embankment.

At the end of the 'tunnel', go over the stile into a field and keep straight on between the LH fence and the RH ridge.   At the end of the fence, with the private lakes down on your left and an enclosed wood 100 yards up on your right, aim to the right of the solitary oak tree in front of you.   After the tree, you will see a sheep track aiming straight towards a small group of trees and another sheep track veering slightly right. Follow the right direction, then aim for the cottage roof which appears ahead of you. Finally, aim for the stile in the wire fence at the far side of the field.

Over the stile, follow the fence round to the next stile and go over into the concrete yard of Pound Farm.   This is a dairy farm with a tall silo and cattle sheds on your right and with dairy buildings on your left as you cross the yard.   Don't linger on your way through.   This is a working farm and you're only on a leisure trip.   Oh yes, you are!   Keep straight on, past turnings down to your left and past tracks between wire fences up on your right, the last of which goes up to unvisitable tumuli.   Then on an uphill, pure white chalk track, go past Pound Farm house on your left.

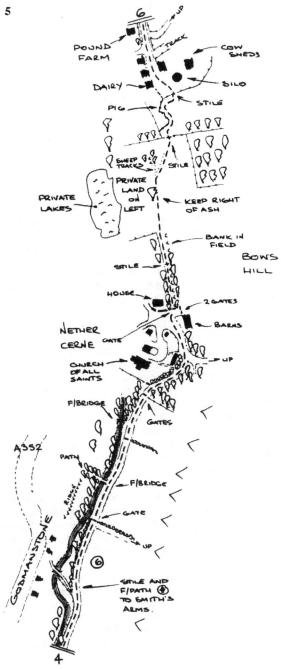

DAY 3 - STAGE 6

POUND FARM TO CERNE ABBAS

Past the bungalow over the LH fence, cross the lower slopes of Green Hill in the open field to a gate in the hedge facing you.   There are water cress beds beyond the farm behind you, down on your left.   Through the gate, the track is still dazzlingly white chalk as you follow it across the next, very long, field towards the foot of Black Hill. The River Cerne still runs along the row of trees down on your left whilst you follow the escarpment on your right for 1/4 mile to the next gate.   At last!   There is an official Footpath arrow on either side of these gateposts.   Follow the direction of the arrow which points towards the top RH corner of this next field, at the foot of the escarpment.

Up in this corner, you will find a hole in the deep hedge and, through the other side, you will find yourself in a hawthorn thicket with a Footpath-signed stile in a wire fence.   Over the stile, turn left and, after 10 or 15 yards, turn away from the fence, up the slope for a few steps.   Here, you will find a post with two Footpath arrows.   Bear left and follow the path along the line of bushes and the fence down on your left for a good 1/4 mile until you come to an opening into the field on your left.   The wire fence continues into trees beyond the opening, bearing right, and you now follow the fence closely for a few yards until you come to another arrowed stile in the fence.   Go over the stile and along a short, downhill path to another stile which leads into an open, downward-sloping field.   From here, you get your first glimpse of Giant Hill on the far side of Cerne Abbas.   Have a short instructive rest before you go on.

In the Domesday Book, Cerne Abbas appears as *Cernelium* and it consisted of 12 parcels of land under titles of *Cerne, Cernel and Cerneli*.   You will shortly be passing the Church of St Mary's in Abbey Street.   This church, of Ham Hill stone and flint banding, was erected by the convent for the town's use in the mid 15th Century to the early 16th Century.   It was considerably altered in 1870.   In the North aisle, a small oak tablet records that "here under lyeth ye body of William Cockeram, gent, a practitioner in phisick and chirurgery, who died the twenty first day of January 1679, aged 43 years and 9 months".   Interestingly, in the register for 1804, it is recorded that Mr Thomas Cockeram died, aged 88.   This was twice the lifespan of his ancestor, William.   Was this with the aid of William's earlier work or by natural means?   Actually, Hutchins reckoned that Cerne Abbas had been distinguished by the longevity of its inhabitants.

At the end of Abbey Street, as you would expect, stand the remains of the Abbey of St Mary, St Peter and St Edwold, said to have been founded by Augustine, but more likely to have been founded about 870 AD by Edwold, brother of St Edmund the Martyr who had been murdered by the Danes.   Edwold died in 871 AD and was interred here. You'll soon find out why you had to bring a laurel leaf.   You didn't forget, did you?

Over the stile, a path follows the edge of the wood around to your right but aim to the right of the allotments instead.   There, you will find a gate which leads onto a fenced drive, past the allotments on the left and past gates and a footpath on the right, into Cerne Abbas.   Follow the track between hedges to an intersection of Chescombe estate roads.   Cross over the first road and keep straight on to the next T-junction with Back Lane.   Turn left and follow the lane down past a hedge and gate on your left and cottages on your right.

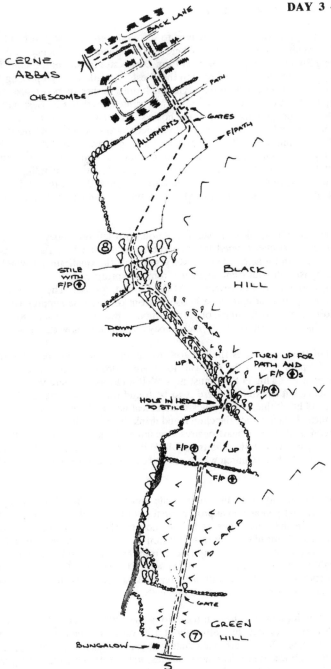

CERNE ABBAS TO GIANT HILL

On down the lane, past cottages and hedges to left and right, follow the bends until you arrive at a telephone box on a grass island. This stands at the junction of Back Lane with Long Street, the main A352 road from Dorchester to Sherborne until it was diverted along the previously minor road to the West. Walk slowly up Long Street and admire the many different building styles including timber framed houses, stone and flint chequered houses, brick-faced and pastel-painted, rendered houses. There is such a fine blend of developing styles in the houses of Cerne Abbas that, with careful maintenance and the addition of a mass of floral decoration by its proud residents, it had no trouble in winning the "Best Kept Large Village" award in 1992. It is still very pretty and particularly clean - so smarten yourself up a bit before you start ambling through. You will also have a choice of watering holes including a couple of teashops, the "New Inn", the "Red Lion" and the "Royal Oak", in that order as you progress, past Puck Street and the fine Manse Cottage behind iron railings on the left, up Long Street.

Past the bus shelter, with the Royal Oak facing you, turn left up Abbey Street and go up the road, past the timber-framed Pitchmarket on your left where farmers used to 'pitch' samples of corn for sale. Past St Mary's church, the small stream which runs in front of the houses on your right emanates from the spring which feeds the village pond in the top corner of Abbey Street. At the far end, go past 'The Barn' and the pond and, with a superb flint and stone house in front of you (the suppressed Abbey provided building materials for much of Cerne Abbas), bear off right and go through the iron gate in the stone wall of the former Abbey churchyard - now the cemetery.

Your route out of the cemetery is the left fork to the other iron gate but, before you leave, follow the path next to the RH wall to where it drops down to about 15 feet below the graveyard. This is St Augustine's Well and this is where you need your laurel leaf, so unpack it carefully. Here is to be found the purest water in the whole district and legend has it that, if you pluck a laurel leaf and make it into a cup and dip it in the well, then stand and face the church and drink the miraculous water, making a wish for something that your heart desires - wishing silently and keeping the wish secret - in time, your wish will come true: Old Wife's report 1935. Presumably, legend means the old Abbey Church which stood beyond the wall with the exit gate, so face that way.

Now, leave the old churchyard by the second gate and keep to the left of the big oak tree on the bank facing you as you approach the foot of Giant Hill. Across the field, go over the stile in the wire fence and don't add to the erosion of the hill by scrambling up the path ahead on your right but turn up the *first* path on your right (but only until you meet another path coming round from the right again) then turn left to follow the slightly uphill path, through initial scrub, to pass the foot of the Giant's National Trust enclosure. If you want a better look at the Giant, follow one of the uphill fences and then come back down to this path.

Follow the faint path (almost a sheep track) along the lower slopes of the hill, with the valley below on your left, but, after about 100 yards, the path fades out and is superseded by a clearer chalky path immediately above it. Change to this upper path and follow it, past a few scrubby hawthorn bushes, until it grows wider and grassier, just like your descending path off the downs into Godmanstone earlier today.

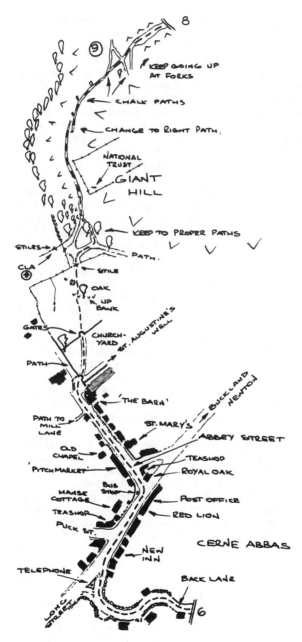

8

⑨

KEEP GOING UP AT FORKS

CHALK PATHS

CHANGE TO RIGHT PATH.

NATIONAL TRUST

GIANT HILL

KEEP TO PROPER PATHS

STILES

PATH.

CLA

STILE

OAK UP BANK

GATES

CHURCH-YARD

ST. AUGUSTINE'S WELL

PATH

'THE BARN'

BUCKLAND NEWTON

PATH TO MILL LANE

ST. MARY'S

ABBEY STREET

OLD CHAPEL

TEASHOP

PITCH MARKET

ROYAL OAK

BUS STOP

MANSE COTTAGE

POST OFFICE

TEASHOP

RED LION

PUCK ST.

CERNE ABBAS

NEW INN

TELEPHONE

BACK LANE

LONG STREET

6

63

DAY 3 - STAGE 8

GIANT HILL TO LITTLE MINTERNE HILL

I thought you might like a reason to stop climbing for a few minutes about here. The views from this slope, across, up and down the valley are superb, whilst the stone mullioned house and the church on the other side of the valley are at UpCerne and are well worth a moments delay. Plus - I haven't told you about the Giant, yet. There are many theories about his arrival here and the reasons for his appearance but, to avoid further guesswork, I'll just quote Hutchins on the subject. "The Giant is attributed to: 1) 'amusement of idle people'. 2) made by Lord Holles' servants (but only repaired by them). 3) the outline of a sleeping giant killed by enraged peasants after he'd eaten some sheep and fallen asleep. or 4) cut at the dissolution in derision of the abbot who had given Queen Emma exile at the Abbey. The indecent appearance is expressive of lust; the uplifted club of his meditated revenge; the position of his feet, the necessity of quitting the place. There you are. You choose.

Now, continue up the path, bearing right and then left through a clearing after which you get your first glimpse of Minterne Magna House (your El Dorado for today). Over a strange ridge, go over the stile in the wire fence ahead of you and, in the flint-filled field - just like the top of Forston Down - aim for the Dutch barn up the field. On your way, you will see a gateway, near the barn. Head for this and, when you arrive, go through the gateway with yellow arrows on both sides of the post, onto a wide, grassy track. Follow the track, between ashes, oaks and a lofty pine on the left and the open field on the right, until the track turns off to the right. On the left, there is a half-gate which leads to the signed Bridleway for Minterne Parva - also signed as Footpath and Wessex Ridgeway. Up the field, your track leads to two gates and a half-gate, again with Footpath and W.R. signs. Here, you have a choice. The quickest and easiest way to cover the 1/2 mile to Little Minterne Hill is along the grass verge on the other side of this road but, if you don't mind a large descent and an equally large ascent to avoid this road, you can cross over into the Caravan Park and follow the Bridleway arrows which start from between the Shower Block and the Chemical Toilet Disposal to the Bridleway which you will meet at a T-junction and then turn left back to the road. Personally, with such a short distance to go and having traversed a few ridges already, I favoured the roadside verge.

So, come with me. Cross to the firm, wide and level verge and turn left along the roadside. Follow it, past a stile into a beech clump on your right and past a couple of gates in opposite hedges. Then, cross to the LH side, along an old oak and sycamore wood at the end of which you go through a small gate with a Bridleway arrow and Bridleway posts as well. The track opposite is the return from the off-road alternative. Through the gate, there is a glorious foretaste of the Vale which awaits you on Day 4. As you bear towards the farm gate in the wire fence over on your right, you will see, far ahead of you, the two sides of the valley and, between these slopes, you will see the plains of Blackmore Vale spread out in the distance.

Today, though, you've only got another mile to go - and it's all downhill. With the valley down on your left and the road hedge over on your right, go through the gate with the Bridleway arrow, into the next field. Follow the LH wire fence, on a level, grand, grassy-smooth stroll and, at the end of this field, you will come to a more used gravel track with grass up the middle. Turn left onto it and follow it, passing a couple of gates on your left and a Bridleway-signed gate in the hedge on your right

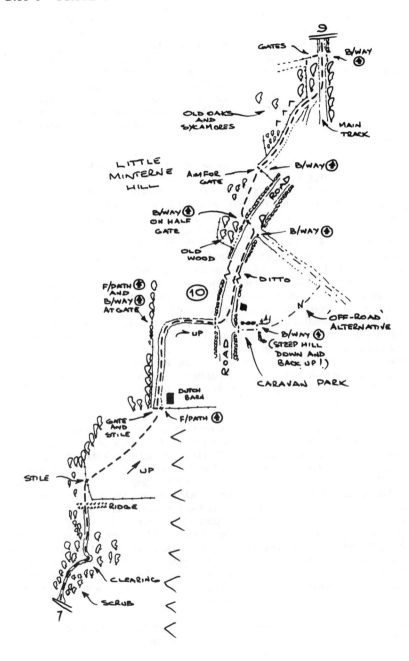

DAY 3 - STAGE 9

LITTLE MINTERNE HILL TO MINTERNE MAGNA

Still enjoying this leisurely stroll, you can see Minterne Magna House down past the tree-clad slopes of Little Minterne Hill. These slopes of ancient oaks and sycamores are part of the ancient lands of the Digby family who have owned, and still own, Minterne Magna, the house and the land since the 1st Sir Everard Digby, the 2nd son of Aelmar, or Almarus who held lands in Tilton, Leicestershire at the time of the Domesday Book in 1086. The Church of St Andrew, where our path arrives in Minterne Magna, is based on Saxon origins but the chancel and the nave were added as recently as the early 15th Century. The North chapel was added in the 16th Century whilst the tower was rebuilt in 1800 and heightened in 1898 during the Church's restoration.

Right, now let's go down there. Keep on along this high track, between a LH fence and RH trees. Through the RH trees, you will glimpse the Blackmore Vale stretching out far below. *Day 4 will be quite an experience.* However, I know you're tired, so plod on, past some tall pines on the left, until you come to some gorse bushes along the track. On the left, you will find a farm gate without any signs or arrows on it. This is where your Bridleway turns off this track. Don't miss it! There aren't any signs for the next few gates, either. Through this gate, aim WNW (60 degrees right) to find a faint, grassy track which runs level along the slopes of the hill. Bear right onto this track and follow a level line along the slopes until you see two small woods down on your left - not too far down. (You may or may not meet a large gate and a small gate across your path on the way. It all depends on whether the incomplete fence I found was being built or was being removed). Anyway, turning downhill between these two small woods, you will find a half-gate, nearer to the RH wood than the LH wood. Go through the gate into a short, scrubby section which leads to a second small gate. Go through this gate as well and go down the field ahead to a third small gate near the end of a wire fence. Now, follow the left-bending fence to a right-turning, downhill path (passing a Bridleway signpost which points back the way you have come to "Buckland Newton", ahead to "Minterne Magna" and left to "Estate Track Only".

Follow the RH wire fence down and take note of the farm gate which leads into the field on your right - This is where you return for Day 4's voyage of discovery. Keep on down along the iron fence and follow the clearer track, through the gate with trees and bushes on the left, around the bend and across a small stream outside the cottage on your left. Use the little bridge if the water's too deep. Then follow the lane around to the right, past the chickens over the RH bank and past gates on either side of the lane. The stone wall on the left is the boundary wall of Minterne Magna House, home of the Digbys. In just 100 yards, you arrive, past a very pretty stone-mullioned cottage, to the A352 with the Church of St Andrew on your right and Minterne Magna House gates around to your left. Do go and visit St Andrew's but be careful - the door at the foot of the tower opens straight onto the main road. Minterne Magna House is open to visitors but as it's so late and you're tired, make a note to pay a visit another time. The gardens are really lovely, packed with unusual plants and with the river running through them.

Well, that's Day 3 finished. Hasn't it been a grand ramble? Let's meet up here for Day 4 - it's completely different. There's lots to see and, as you'll be in Blackmore Vale almost immediately, it's nearly level all day.

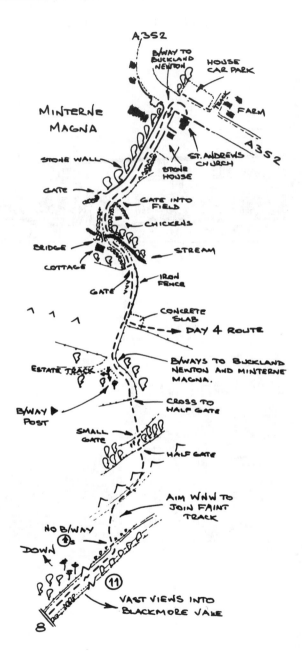

A352

B/WAY TO BUCKLAND NEWTON

HOUSE CAR PARK

FARM

MINTERNE MAGNA

A352

ST. ANDREWS CHURCH

STONE WALL

STONE HOUSE

GATE

GATE INTO FIELD

CHICKENS

BRIDGE

STREAM

COTTAGE

IRON FENCE

GATE

CONCRETE SLAB

DAY 4 ROUTE

ESTATE TRACK

B/WAYS TO BUCKLAND NEWTON AND MINTERNE MAGNA.

B/WAY POST

CROSS TO HALF GATE

SMALL GATE

HALF GATE

AIM WNW TO JOIN FAINT TRACK

NO B/WAYs

DOWN

(11)

8

VAST VIEWS INTO BLACKMORE VALE

TOP: UPBURY FARM, YETMINSTER - PAGE 80

BOTTOM: BARWICK HOUSE, BARWICK - PAGE 86

DAY 4 - INTRODUCTION

MINTERNE MAGNA TO YEOVIL

And now, as they say, for something completely different. Day 3 was quite strenuous with the climb up to the Dorset Downs from Dorchester, followed by the ups and downs from one ridge to another and back. Today, we have pleasant country lanes leading you through lovely Dorset villages which could fill, single-handed, many books on cottage garden plants and weighty tomes on vernacular architecture.

After the initial wooded lane which goes over the end of High Stoy ridge, from where you will have the most enticing views into The Blackmore Vale, you descend into the plains where cattle and sheep are the main occupants. As Hutchins recounts, "Farms are almost entirely appropriated to dairies, and large quantities of butter are weekly sent from hence to the London market". The high, flint-filled downs of the cereal crops have been left behind and the soil is mainly good, rich clay with a narrow ridge of limestone, called corn-brash - an easily worked building stone - in the Yetminster area. As a result, there are some lovely stone-built cottages and more noble buildings on today's walk. There are village shops, inns and wonderful old churches to visit. There are small farms galore, flower-bedecked lanes and ancient tracks. There are wide grassy fields and shady woods. We're off to the land of the Yetties and to see the fascinating dairy cottage where the deadly smallpox met its Waterloo. And there's a fine collection of follies to be seen in the Park of Barwick House near the end of the Day. Quite a programme, so, "Let's go to Yeovil!"

	STAGE	MILES	TOTAL MILES
1.	Minterne Magna to High Stoy	1.50	1.50
2.	High Stoy to White House Common	2.25	3.75
3.	White House Common to Leigh	1.25	5.00
4.	Leigh to Herbury Lane	1.50	6.50
5.	Herbury Lane to Yetminster	0.75	7.25
6.	Yetminster to The Meadows	1.00	8.25
7.	The Meadows to Clifton Farm	1.50	9.75
8.	Clifton Farm to Yeovil Junction	0.50	10.25
9.	Yeovil Junction to Two Tower Lane	1.25	11.50
10.	Two Tower Lane to Yeovil	0.75	12.25

Oh, yes. By the way, you're also going to the village where the last witch to have been burned at the stake in the whole of England was arrested. This is, of course, deepest, darkest Dorset.

DAY 4 - STAGE 1

MINTERNE MAGNA TO HIGH STOY

Arriving back in Minterne Magna, go down the lane between the Church and The House back to the gate at the end of the iron fence which I pointed out on your arrival (Stage 9, penultimate paragraph).

Turn left through this gate and, with the wire fence on your right at first, aim for the RH side of the solitary oak tree.   Here, pick up the narrow path, probably a sheep track, and follow it under a low ash and keep straight on along the path until you come to a gate in the fence across your route.   At the gate, aim for the RH end of the house which appears ahead of you and, when you arrive at the hedged house, go through the Bridleway-arrowed farm gate on its right.

Be careful when you reach the roadside and turn right onto the RH verge of the A352. In a few yards, the verge runs out at the banked trees and the sweep of the road makes it better to cross over to the left.   In just a few more yards, turn up the LH-turning lane where the road sign points to "Leigh 3" and "Yetminster 6".   This is the long, wooded lane to High Stoy and, as you follow the end of this ridge with the high banked ancient sycamores on your left, the RH bank eventually becomes lower and allows you to see into The Blackmore Vale.   But first, enjoy the cool shade of the trees and the smell of garlic, if it's the right time of year.   At a double gate on your right, where a farm track hairpins its way down the end of the ridge, stop for a few moments to savour the panorama of small fields, deep pasture, peace and quiet which is the Oxford Clay land of "The Vale" spread out below you.   I could wax eloquent here but perhaps I'll leave it to Hutchins who says about the view from High Stoy...."one of the most beautiful and extensive prospects to be seen in Dorset.   The whole of the North side of Dorset and a great part of Somerset as far as Mendip is spread under your feet like a map and there are extensive views of South and West Dorset".   There now.

At a right-angled sweep bend in the road, where a deep hollow-way goes up on your left into the deep recesses of Penn Wood, you emerge into the light of a downhill view straight ahead.   Now, with lower, hedged fields on either side, a Footpath-signed stile next to a gate on your left leads onto the North-West slopes of High Stoy.   However, keep straight on down, past a new wood on the left and a gate on the right opposite a large oak.

You may have already noticed that the hedgerows hold an unusually large quantity of ancient oaks.   These are remnants of the medieval forests which covered all of this clay-based flatland.   Over the hundreds of years between then and now, the forests have been cleared, with a few exceptional small woods remaining, but odd trees have been left where lines of hedges have been planted to bound the myriad of fields of the Blackmore Vale and its surrounding hills.

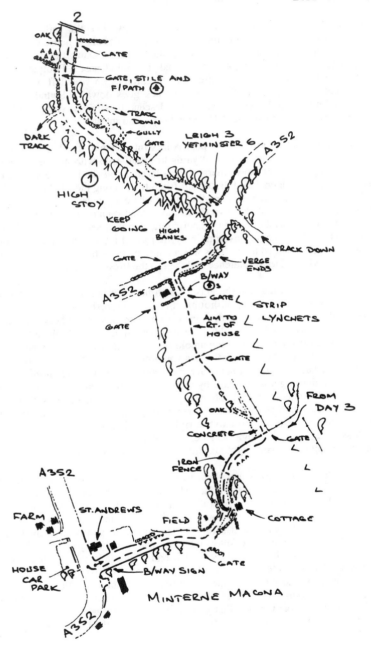

DAY 4 - STAGE 2

HIGH STOY TO WHITE HOUSE COMMON

On a short level stretch of the lane, there are good views into the valley on the left and into the Vale on the right until, after gates on both sides and a house with a beech hedge on the right, the lane goes up and over a small rise.   Down the other side, go under the outstretched branches of opposite oak trees and past a Footpath-arrowed stile next to a gate on the RH side.   After hedged cottages on your left, with another signed Footpath stile opposite, the next left track goes down to Pound Farm with another hedged house on the RH corner.   Still descending slightly, you come to a left sweep bend in the road whilst your RH hedge keeps straight on.

On the bend, a Bridleway arrow on a post points into a small thicket on the right corner.   Plunge into this thicket for 10 yards to a half-gate with another Bridleway arrow on its gatepost.   You now emerge into a large, open field where you turn left and follow a wide, fence-enclosed, hoofprint-filled track along the LH hedge.   At the end of the fence, you emerge into a small clearing where a gate leads out into the road through Hermitage.   The gate has two Bridleway arrows on a post inside the field and one outside in the lane whilst, down on your right, you will see a telephone box and the village hall.   Hermitage, unsurprisingly, is named after 'a hermitage or priory which was anciently founded here. This was a house of Friar hermits of St Augustine and it was first dedicated to St Laurence and then to the Blessed Virgin Mary'.

Now, cross the road, bearing into the grassy patch between hedges on the other side. There are no Bridleway arrows although this is Stonerush Drove and the deep hoofprints in the Oxford Clay beneath your feet confirm that many horses come this way.   If it's wet, look out for muddy, wet patches - if it's dry, look out for your ankles.   This track is confined between an old wood on the right and the edge of the wood before a fenced field on your left.   As you progress along 3/4 mile of track, you are following the edge of a parish boundary, marked by the earth bank along the edge of the wood.   You can guess at its age by the size of the trees growing in it.   Cross a minor track which comes in from a half-gate on your left and, later, pass a farm gate and, later still, pass another half-gate.   Eventually, there is a very wide, deep ditch on your right and, when it bears off to the right, you will find a small gate in a wire fence across your path.   Through the gate, you are in a wide field with fenced hedges continuing straight on on your right and running away to your left.

There are no Bridleway arrows anywhere to be seen so pay close attention to these directions: You want to arrive at the far LH end of this field but there are no paths visible.   The Bridleway actually goes straight on from this gate until, close to the power line post which faces you, our route turns left along another Bridleway running slightly North of due West but, as I said, there are no signs and no used paths that I could see.   If the field is planted, follow whatever path is cut for you, around the edge or through the middle of the field, to the far LH end of the field where, 30 yards from the RH corner which has a few trees crowded into it, you will find a small steel gate. Through this gate, aim to the left of the single tree which stands in the field, over on your right.   As you approach the tree, you will see a gate in the low hedge down on your left.   Now turn off towards that gate and, when you have crossed the plank bridge over the ditch on the other side, aim up to the gate in the hedge above you.

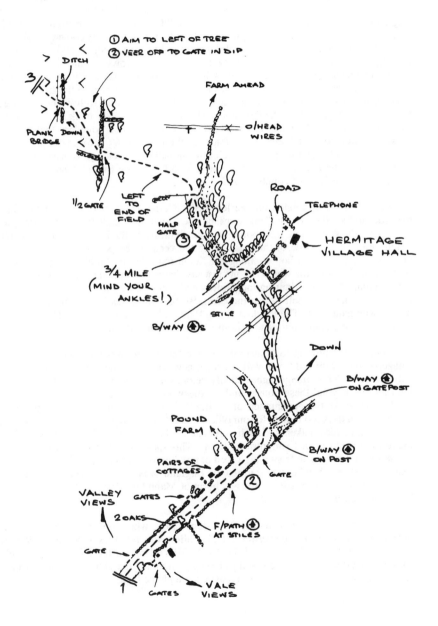

① AIM TO LEFT OF TREE
② VEER OFF TO GATE IN DIP

DITCH

3

PLANK DOWN BRIDGE

1/2 GATE

LEFT TO END OF FIELD

HALF GATE

3/4 MILE (MIND YOUR ANKLES!)

B/WAY ④s

③

FARM AHEAD

O/HEAD WIRES

ROAD

TELEPHONE

HERMITAGE VILLAGE HALL

STILE

DOWN

B/WAY ④ ON GATE POST

ROAD

POUND FARM

B/WAY ④ ON POST

PAIRS OF COTTAGES

GATE

②

VALLEY VIEWS

GATES

F/PATH ④ AT STILES

2 OAKS

GATE

1

GATES

VALE VIEWS

WHITE HOUSE COMMON TO LEIGH

Stand at this top gate for a while and get your bearings.   There is a high hedge on the LH side of the field and a deep row of old trees facing you at the other end.   There is a single tree standing in the field.   Your exit from this field is not clear from here but it consists of a small gap in the trees, about 100 yards from the far LH corner.   The best way to find it is to go down the LH side of the field to the far corner and then follow the edge of the wood until you find the opening.   The cows go into this wood for shade so there are openings before yours but yours is unmistakable because you can see a wooden bridge across the very wide ditch when you peer into the trees.   Go through the two small gates on either end of the bridge and follow the enclosed Bridleway (no signs) along the RH edge of this field.   The earth bank, on which the RH old oaks are standing, appears to be part of the same parish boundary that we met earlier.   After a dry ditch crosses the track, go through the gate across your path onto a wide, grassy, clay and flint track which runs into an open field on your right.   All of the trees in the hedges are oaks on the left and ashes on the right until the track arrives at a T-junction of country lanes.

The main road swings round from the left from "Cerne Abbas 5.3/4" whilst the right turn goes to "Sherborne 5.3/4" and our lane goes down to "Leigh 1/12 and Yetminster 3".   Past the stone-mullioned house on your right, begin the long, easy descent into Leigh along the RH side of the road, using the verge when possible.   There are so many fine cottages and houses along the Leigh road that it would be impossible to point them all out on the way so let me just say that you should take the time to amble slowly along the lane, admiring the gardens and cottages as you go.   Take note of the large number of small farms, including Bridge Farm, Iles Farm, Cross Farm and houses with names like The Paddock, Long Barn and Orchard House.   This is still a thriving farming community and it hasn't all been 'converted'.

Just after the LH turning to "Batcombe 3" and the bridge over the stream before the garage/shop on your right, you will see some new houses on the left with a street sign "Miz Maze".   This strange name actually belongs to an even stranger spot.   It is on high ground beyond these houses and, in the words of another local 'Old Wife of 1935'..."presents the appearance of a slightly raised, flat mound, some paces in diameter.   In days too remote for our oldest inhabitants to recall, it was the meeting place of the holiday makers of Leigh.   As late as the year 1800 the Maze existed, in the form of banks made to an intricate form.   This spot was a noted gathering place of witches as it was remote from a high road or any big town or village.   Tradition has it that the last witch who was burned in England was arrested when attending a conference in the Miz-Maze".   She was burnt at Maumbury Rings, Dorchester in the late 17th Century.

Now, continue down the road and, at the village cross, where the right fork takes the busier road directly to "Yetminster 2.1/2", follow the left fork towards "Chetnole 1.1/2".   Pass School Cottage and the 1833 Village Hall on the left and the lovely Cromwell Cottage on your right and just keep going until the church appears in view after Orchard House on your right, opposite a telephone box.

THE BLACKMORE VALE PATH

DAY 4 - STAGE 3

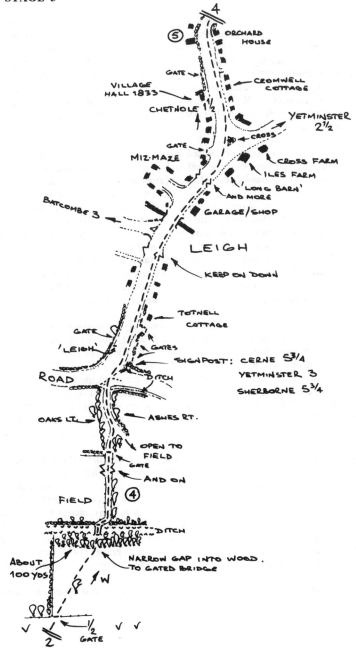

LEIGH TO HERBURY LANE

Just past Orchard House, a narrow path goes off to the right leading to the Parish Church of St Andrew. Yes, another one. This is because this church, and another at Ryme Intrinseca, was originally a chapel belonging to the Church of St Andrew at Yetminster - all belonging to the Bishop of Salisbury at the end of the 11th Century and the beginning of the 12th. This lovely little church, in the Perpendicular style, has a waggon-type wooden roof resting on carved stone bosses whilst the three cinque-foil lights of the West window contain beautiful stained glass representations of the Crucifixion, St Mary and St John. There are some rather smart gargoyles on the outside of the aisle.

Leaving by either of the churchyard gates, keep following the lane through Leigh, past a twin-gabled house on the left and past the left turn after it, opposite Willow Tree Farm. Having passed several small farms with entrances onto this lane already, there are still several more to come. After the "Carpenters' Arms" on your right (or via the "Carpenters' Arms" on your right), keep on going, past Leigh Farm, Frampton Farm and Brookside Farm and, after a thatched cottage over on the left, past Fudge's the Bakers on the edge of the brook. The long ribbon of cottages and farms has now begun to thin out a little and, from the corner of the next turning on the right, Alton Mead Lane, I was going to take you across the field Footpath to Yetminster. However, the path appears to have been obliterated so we will carry on along the road for another 1/2 mile to a comfortable track and Bridleway. Never mind, it's not that long before you turn off and it's quite easy along the road.

After the houses on the left before the "Leigh" sign, the road bends left with a ditch on the RH side and, beyond the stone-walled Park House Farm on your left, you have just 200 yards to go before you leave civilisation for a while. You pass a couple of farm gates in the RH hedge and, immediately afterwards, turn right onto a gravely path, Herbury Lane, between hedges and with grass up the middle. You will have noticed the changes beneath your feet during the first part of today's walk. Having left behind the flint and the chalk, you are now on gravel-rich soil which, being rich and well drained, supports cattle galore and many dairy farms, as you have seen already.

After two ash trees, there are two opposing farm gates, the RH one having a stile with a Footpath arrow. This leads across to the Footpath which I wanted to use but we're too far towards Yetminster for it to be any use now. So keep straight on, past another LH gate and a RH grass track. There are several old trees dotted along the hedges and their shade is welcome on hot days as is their shelter on damp days. At two more opposing gates, the LH one has a Footpath arrow this time and there's another one a little further on. Ignore them all until, at opposite farm gates where the high-hedged track ahead becomes completely grass, both gates carry Footpath arrows and the RH one is arriving from the corner of Alton Mead Lane in Leigh..

Keep straight on, past the first old oak tree, into the banked Bridleway (unmarked).

THE BLACKMORE VALE PATH

DAY 4 - STAGE 4

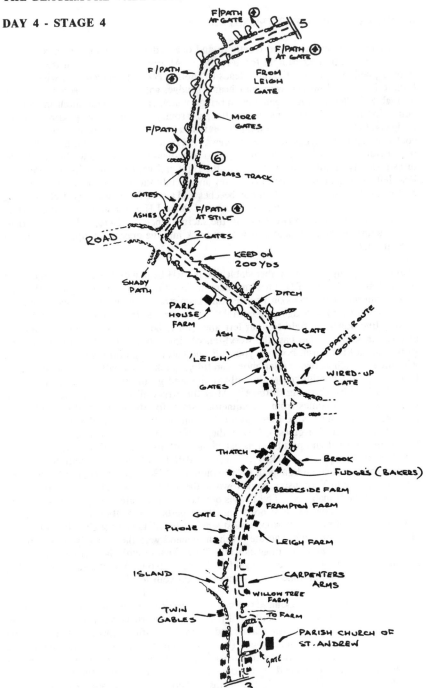

DAY 4 - STAGE 5

HERBURY LANE TO YETMINSTER

Now enclosed between banked hawthorn and oak hedges, the track zig-zags left and right before continuing straight for 1/4 mile. At a wider section, with trees on the right, a plank bridge over the ditch leads to another Footpath-signed stile which leads back to Leigh. However, we won't bear a grudge, will we? Just keep straight on, through a Bridleway-signed gate onto a bridge which crosses a wide ditch in front of you. In this scrubby clearing, follow the path round left and right, passing another bridge and Footpath lurking on the left, until you arrive at a fork where the Footpath continues up to the right and our Bridleway forks left. Go through the gate, with both Bridleway and Footpath arrows, onto a hedged-in track where the Bridleway turns instantly uphill between hedges to the right and we leave it to its own devices. Bear left to the gate with a Footpath arrow and go into the long, narrow field beyond. Follow the LH, banked line of stubby beeches and a wire fence, with the field sloping up on your right to a line of trees and bushes. Past a LH gate and a RH cattle trough, go over the stile next to two gates in the facing fence. Here, a Footpath arrow points across the concrete and tarmac farm track into the grass track opposite, known as Mill Lane.

There are steps up to some timber stables on the RH bank with bushes along the track on the left. After a RH-intruding barn makes the path zig-zag, ignore the dog hurling himself at the gates on your left and keep straight on, with a wooden fence on your left and a banked hedge on your right. You can see the Dorchester-Yeovil main railway line down the field to your left and you'll be crossing it soon (on an un-manned crossing). Go past the wood-fenced, low stone-built Mill House and the stone-walled Mill Farm, both on your left and carefully go through the barrier gate with the Footpath arrow. Even more carefully, quickly and without a sound in case there's anything coming, cross the railway line and go through the identical gate on the other side by Crossing Cottage. After the River Wriggle bridge (quaint little name, isn't it? - It comes from the numerous small fossilised stems of crinoids, sea-growing plants which were found at the bottom of the brook and which the local inhabitants called "Wriggles"), follow the tarmac lane, past a field on the left and houses on the right and past St Francis Cottage with its stone walls on the left facing a hedged field opposite. Near the top of Mill Lane, the stone wall on the left supports high ground and the path to "Chetnole 2". Here, at a sweeping bend in the road, you arrive in Yetminster, home town of the Yetties. No, not the elusive, furry creatures of the Himalayas. The Yetties of whom I speak are not in the least shy or reticent. Just in case you're not from 'these parts', the Yetties are Dorset's most famous quartet of musicians who, almost single-handed, have kept alive the traditions of Dorset folk singing and who are much in demand with their acutely observed and highly entertaining modern songs as well. "An Evening with the Yetties" should be sampled whenever or wherever you get the chance. Now, continue into Yetminster, past the fine, stone-mullioned Greystones over on your left.

Yetminster appears in the Domesday Book as *Etiminstre*, belonging to the Bishop of Salisbury and containing one mill. In AD 1091, the Bishop certified that he had built a new church at Sarum and that he had endowed it with the town of Eteminster and the knights' fees of the land there (to help support Sarum). This being The Blackmore Vale Path, it is fitting that we are now entering this small town because it is conjectured that "its name derives from Gateminster and this was the principle gate into the Forest of Blakemore - Ryme Intrinseca being a postern gate": Hutchins.

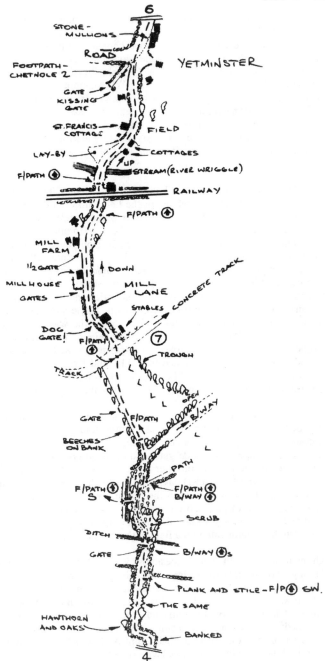

79

YETMINSTER TO THE MEADOWS

The next stone barn on your right carries a Blue Plaque commemorating the birth of Benjamin Jesty in Upbury Farm opposite. To look through that gate and across the farmyard to the old, much used and extended farm cottage is almost to step back to the time when Jesty lived there. The plaque says he was born in 1736 but his tombstone, in the graveyard of St Nicholas' Church, Worth Matravers in Purbeck, says that he died on 16th April 1816, aged 70. What cannot be in doubt is that he was instrumental in preventing untold numbers of deaths from smallpox. I'll let the inscription on his tombstone speak for him - "Benjamin Jesty, born at Yetminster in this County, was an upright and honest man; particularly noted for having been the person (known) that introduced the cow-pox by inoculation, and who from his strength of mind made the experiment from the cow on his wife and two sons in the year 1774".

Now, follow the footpath along Jesty's boundary wall to the Church of St Andrew. Originally Norman, the church was rebuilt in the late 13th Century and again in the 16th Century in Perpendicular style. It has a waggon(or barrel)-type roof with some original ancient coloured decoration. A sympathetic restoration was carried out in the late 19th Century. Leaving by the twin wrought-iron gates, continue along the road, past the Church Hall and the Rectory on the left. There are still some fine local limestone houses on your way through to the next T-junction (where you turn left) and beyond. Keep looking as you pass Oak House Stores, not forgetting to buy something, and carry on past Field House, the Post Office and the Veterinary Surgeon opposite. On the way out of Yetminster, straight on, Boyle's School stands on the right. This was founded by Robert Boyle (1627-1691) who was born in Ireland but inherited the manor of Stalbridge in the centre of Blackmore Vale whilst still young. Boyle became a scientist and specialised in experiments with pneumatics. This school was endowed by Boyle and opened in 1711 - and I've no doubt that the poor unfortunates would have been taught the law of relationship between pressure and volume of gases known to all as "Boyle's Law". Remember it? No, nor me.

However, that's beyond our path so, at Petties Farm on the right, turn into their farmyard by the Footpath-arrowed post. Go through four farm gates straight on as you pass through the yard, with private car parking and farm sheds. After the fourth gate, follow the LH hedge, past a side gate, and cross an open field with an ancient field system of ridges and furrows on your left. The next stile, which is straight across and between a LH ash and a RH oak, has a Footpath arrow. Go straight across this last field to another arrowed stile in the hedge, over which you turn left onto a rubble and gravel track with grass up the middle. At the end of the track, turn left onto the road and, past 'Journey's End', turn right at the Footpath arrow on the verge post and go through the farm gate into a field with a hedge on your left.

Go through the next gate in the wire fence across your path and go straight across the next field to a gate in the opposite hedge. Over the gate, turn sharp right and follow the RH hedge and a faint path to another gate and a stile in the far RH corner. The gate has painted arrows on both sides. Over this stile, you are in a very open field with intruding lines of hedges. Bear slightly left and aim for the stile about 100 yards along the LH hedge. Over this stile, again with a faint painted arrow, cross the open field to the right of the solitary large oak (approx. North-East) or, if the field is planted, go round the edge in an anti-clockwise direction.

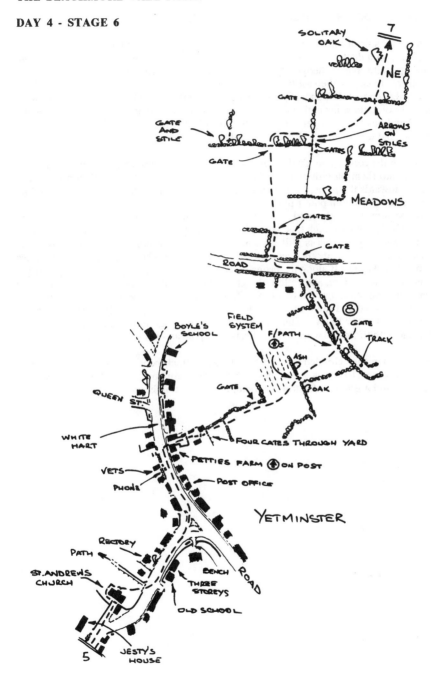

THE MEADOWS TO CLIFTON MAYBANK

On the far side of this field, between two willows, you will find a stile and a wooden bridge over a ditch.   On the other side, keep straight on to a gate between two oaks in the opposite angled hedge, again with a ditch.   Through this gate, take a few moments to survey the vast field on the other side.   There is a gate half-way along the hedge on your left and, after this hedge turns off left, making the field extra wide at that point, there is another gate in the far distant LH corner.   Ignore the rest of the field and head for this gate in a North-North-West direction.   There are still no arrows, but don't worry.   It's quite alright.

Through the corner gate, go through a narrow wood, or thick row of trees, with paths going into them on either side.   In the next wide field, a faint path aims straight across towards the painted farmhouse, passing an electricity pole, a large oak and an overhead cables high power pylon, all on your LH side.   There is also a small wood over on your left, in the field.   As you cross the field, a farm gate will appear in the facing hedge and, through this, you will see a "Keep Dogs on Lead" sign.   See, I told you it was alright - this is still a Public Footpath.   Joining a soil track across the field, you arrive at another gate in the facing hedge where the main track comes through and turns off along the hedge on your right.   Go through the gate, passing a gate in the RH corner, and follow the gravel farm track for about 100 yards into and past the farm buildings and barns of Clifton Farm.   After the buildings, the track is tarmac-covered and there are two gates on the left leading into the yard and a wire-fenced field.   The RH wire fence leads to a wood fence and the hedged garden of a farm cottage with trimmed lawns and a collection of pine and hardwood trees.

Keep on down the elevated lane, past a LH, gated track between the wire-fenced field and a hedge and RH turns to garages and "Clifton Farmhouse".   After a left bend in the lane and a gate into the low RH field, just keep straight on.

THE BLACKMORE VALE PATH

DAY 4 - STAGE 7

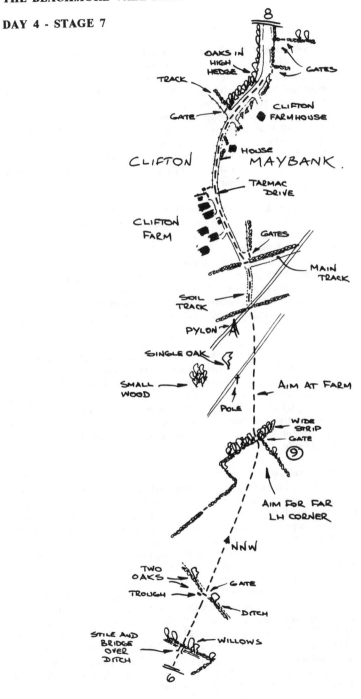

CLIFTON MAYBANK TO YEOVIL JUNCTION

After a LH gate and a collection of farm buildings on your right, the lane runs out at a T-junction with the road. There is a small wood of old oaks and sycamores on your left as you begin a stroll along the road towards the LH bend ahead of you. There is a ditch between the hedge and field fence on your right and, after a wood-fenced turning to a track and the field on the right, both with gates, the road takes a left turn. A high stone barn on the LH corner stands opposite a wire-fenced, square, embanked and levelled field which is all that remains of Clifton Maubank's bowling green, described in a 1648 document as "with fower walks about it, sett with all sorts of fruit, and out of it into the fields there are large walks under tall *elmes* orderly planted". Past the field, a stone wall leads up the RH turning to the gates and high brick boundary wall of Clifton Maubank House.

Clifton Maybank, the manor, dates back to the Domesday Book where it appears as *Clistone* - held by William Malbank from Earl Hugh. The name comes from the original Maubank of the Norman era, an heiress of whom married one of the Horseys. The House remains the seat of the Horsey family but this fine, Ham-stone mullioned building is now the only surviving wing of the original. At the dissolution, the Horseys were granted the Abbey and its grounds and appurtenances, which they didn't waste much time in selling to Sherborne. There is a small, fenced, open wood in the low corner of the next field which contains several sycamores and poplars whilst, beyond the field, there stands a square, brick summer house on the end of the boundary wall.

Now, past turnings into thatched "Clifton Maybank Cottage" and past the cattle grid of the RH House drive, keep on up the inclined road, between hedges, until you reach two stiles, one each side of the road. The one on the left comes from Clifton Farm - but I wanted you to see the front of Clifton Maubank House. The stile in the hedge on the right carries a signpost for Public Footpaths to "Yeovil Junction 1/2 and Yetminster 2". Go over the RH stile into the (*elm-less*) Park of Clifton Maubank House and head across the upper slopes towards the trees in the top, far LH corner - brushing against the RH side of the trunk of the biggest oak of all.

Over the stile, (there's a yellow arrow on the other side) go straight across the field to the other side (or, if the field is planted, go round the RH edge, beyond which there is a very steep drop). Opposite your entry stile, you'll find another stile with a Footpath arrow in the British Rail wire fence. Go over the stile and turn instantly left to follow the wire-enclosed Footpath for about 100 yards. Bearing right, this path descends, past a Footpath arrow on a post, to join a road which runs to the service area on this side of the rail tracks. Join this road down, past the LH Footpath which runs down to the gate into the valley on your left, and go through the stone-walled tunnel under the railway embankment. After the gate on the other side, turn left along the road from Yeovil Junction Station back on your right. Follow the road along the wire-fenced, oak and sycamore-bedecked drop on the RH side and past the bridge which carries the river under the road. At the end, with factory units on the right and the sign for "Yeovil Junction" on the LH corner, carefully cross the road just before it goes under the railway bridge on the left. Take the opposite "Barwick 1/2m" signed path, past the post-box, to "Quarry Cottages" and go up the three steps between the end of the RH hedge and the LH gardens. Bear right and follow the footpath past the end cottage and up into the allotments.

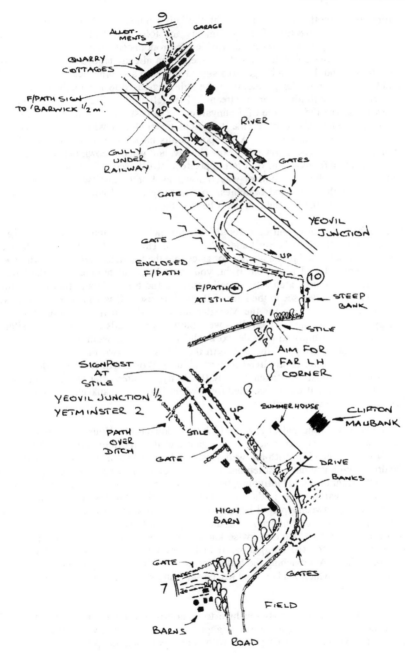

DAY 4 - STAGE 9

YEOVIL JUNCTION TO TWO TOWER LANE

Before taking another step, I must thank the lady from Quarry Cottages who showed me the view from the top of the allotments and told me all about Barwick House (which you will pass very soon - and which is pronounced *Barrick*).   It's the little interludes like these which can add so much to an already enjoyable walk.   Now, begin to descend, between hedges to a signed stile into a sloping field.   Go down the field to the stile in the hedge and, over the stile, zig-zag down through the trees to a wooden-railed footbridge over the stream.   Bear left and then right again to go up the grassy track past the LH side of a bungalow.   Go past a Footpath arrow on the LH post before a short hedge and up the steep field, under electric wires, to a gate and stile in the facing wooden fence.   A signpost points back to "Yeovil Junction 1/2m".   Turn left onto the lane, known as Rexes Hollow, and wander down between hedges to a turning into a farmyard on your left opposite a 'Road used as a Public Footpath' on your right.   This is a hollow-way, known as Long Lane, which is frequently overgrown with nettles and brambles, so don't use it.   Keep straight on, past a wooden gate into the RH field, to a left bend in the lane.

Just on the bend, turn right onto the drive with the stone gateposts which is signed "Public Footpath - Two Tower Lane 1/2m, Yeovil 1m".   Follow the drive, between wire-fenced fields and past a plethora of gates into the LH fields and a small wood with a lake beyond it.   Up on your right, you can't help but notice "Jack the Treacle Eater's Arch" - a rustic arch with a small figure on the top.   This is the first of three follies which you will see in the Park of Barwick House.   It is named after Jack, who ran messages to London for the Messiter family and who liked eating treacle for energy.   Local people say the follies were built in the 1820s by George Messiter of Barwick House simply to provide work whilst the local glovemaking industry was depressed but paintings of the House in the 1780s show two of the follies already there.   The Messiter family lived at Barwick until World War II when, after housing evacuees, the House was taken over by the Army.   Later, after use as a school for juvenile offenders, it was unoccupied for a while but now, thankfully restored, it has been turned into very smart flats.

After a huge, old lime and a LH gate which leads down to the House and the lake, with an arrowed post on the corner, go past a gate into the RH field and immediately turn off the drive over a Footpath-arrowed stile.   More or less maintain the direction of the drive which you have just left and aim to the left of the large lime tree up the field, just to the right of the LH intruding, fenced enclosure.   This line leads you to another signed stile, next to a gate in the wire fence.   Over this stile, take careful aim towards the far hedge, between a pair of large lime trees and a single, twisted beech tree (this looks like a pine tree from here).   On the way across, look away to your left and you will see Messiter's Cone (otherwise known as the Rose Tower) whilst, up on your right, you will see the straight-sided Fish Tower which once bore a fish-shaped weather vane.   Approaching the hedge, nearer the single tree, you will find another stile by a gate which leads onto Two Tower Lane whilst a signpost points back to "Barwick 3/4m".

Go over the stile and cross the lane to a Footpath-arrowed kissing gate in the opposite hedge.   Through the gate, signposted "Yeovil 3/4m", you will find yourself in an equestrian events park, packed with permanent horse jump obstacles.

86

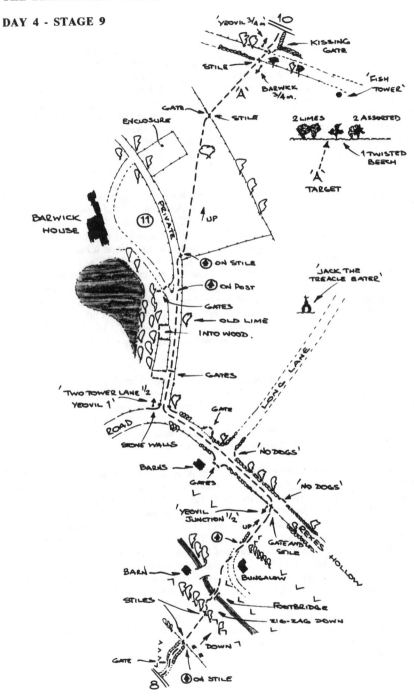

TWO TOWER LANE TO YEOVIL

Following the RH hedge, you arrive at another arrowed kissing gate which leads you onto the upper, scrub-covered slopes of the downs above Nine Springs and Yeovil. Bear left for a couple of yards and then descend, past a ditch-jump and past more open, grassy areas to left and right, towards the tree-filled valley below.   Go between bushes at the bottom and you'll arrive at a kissing gate.   Turn right onto the wide track which runs alongside a split-paling fence bordering the well-trained stream on your left.   Follow the path through trees, with the hill sloping up on your right and with the entrained stream forming several waterfalls and a small lake between gravel paths below you.   After a LH stile into the valley, you arrive at a very large lake with willows and oaks on its edge and with ducks loudly proclaiming their rights.

The track becomes level gravel about here so keep following it down and, after a metal gate and a kissing gate, there is an excellent playground down on your left. Stay on the main track, past "New Walk Cottage" and some benches.   After two gates leading into a barn area on your right, the track joins a tarmac section of lane which comes in from the factory estate ahead of you and runs up around a hairpin to the Ski Centre on the right.   The stream disappears under the road and re-emerges behind bushes on your right, entrained between concrete banks, as you continue walking down the main track.   This is just straight, easy walking, with fenced factories on your left and with trees and the fenced stream between you and the slopes of Summer House Hill on your right for the next 1/4 mile until you reach the Old Railway Station car park off, strangely enough, Old Station Road.   The Toilet block, which is over on your left, is built on the site of the old 1860 station.   This was closed in 1967 and demolished in 1973.

Well, you've arrived in Yeovil, Somerset.   Oh, didn't I mention it?   The Dorset-Somerset border runs along the river which goes under the lane up to the railway station at Yeovil Junction.   In fact, Yeovil Junction station is in Dorset.

As I was saying, you're in Yeovil and Day 5 starts here, in the vicinity of the Toilets. Better make that near the bus shelters on the other side.

Yeovil is listed variously in the Domesday Book as *Givele, Givela, Ivle* and *Ivla,* held by the Count of Mortain and Amund from him.   Also mentioned are Hugh and William d'Eu.   Yeovil takes its name from the River Yeo which runs along its Eastern border. There is evidence of inhabitation by Neolithic man and Bronze-age occupation of Wyndham Hill (where we leave Yeovil on Day 5), Iron-age and Roman settlements. There was a Saxon church here as far back as 950 AD.   After Henry VIII's suppression of religious houses of 1538, the Horseys of Clifton Maubank became Lords of Yeovil but, by 1611, the manorial rights were acquired by Sir Edward Phelips, Master of the Rolls and Speaker of the House of Commons.   This was the builder of Montacute House, about 4 miles West of Yeovil and now owned by the National Trust.

This is a good resting place for Blackmore Vale Path travellers and a quick visit to the Tourist Information Centre by the Civic Offices off Hendford (There's a Town Map outside the Toilets in this car park) will provide all you need for accommodation and details of places to visit.

DAY 4 - STAGE 10

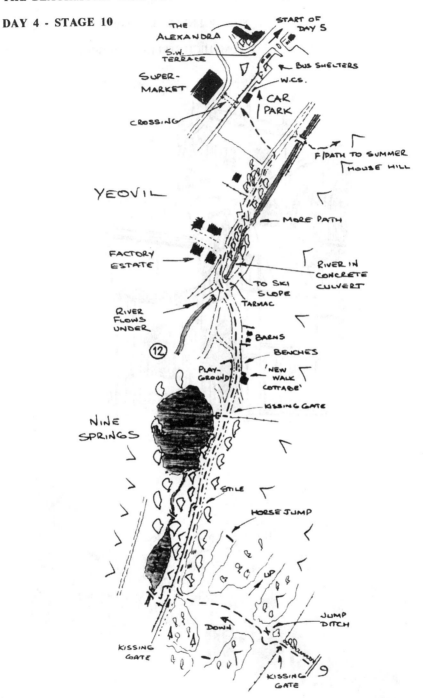

THE BLACKMORE VALE PATH

TOP: SHERBORNE ABBEY, SHERBORNE - PAGE 100

BOTTOM: HIGH STREET, STALBRIDGE - PAGE 112

DAY 5 - INTRODUCTION

YEOVIL TO STALBRIDGE

Leaving Yeovil in Somerset, today's route is, more or less, due East. It begins by leading you through a narrow, sandstone gorge which has appeared in several geological works and, after walking along a low ridge with fine views into Blackmore Vale (and where rival supporters of Roundheads and Cavaliers had a skirmish during the Civil Wars), you will have a most enjoyable, level stroll through fertile meadows to Sherborne. This is a most beautiful town with a historical culture of learning, passed down from the Benedictine monks who originally worshipped at the glorious, mellow stone Abbey which seems out of all proportion to the size of the town. Through Sherborne, an easy walk through the Capability Brown designed Park of Sherborne Castle gives you superb views of Sir Walter Raleigh's magnificent Elizabethan home - now owned by the ever-present Digbys. Our route passes an old hunting lodge in the Park and, on a more thoughtful note, goes through woods which housed an American Army Hospital during World War II.

	STAGE	MILES	TOTAL MILES
1.	Yeovil to Golf Club	1.00	1.00
2.	Golf Club to Roman Site	1.00	2.00
3.	Roman Site to Silverlake Farm	1.75	3.75
4.	Silverlake Farm to Lenthay Road	1.25	5.00
5.	Lenthay Road to Sherborne Station	1.00	6.00
6.	Sherborne Station to Sherborne Park	1.25	7.25
7.	Sherborne Park to Haydon	0.75	8.00
8.	Haydon to Rue Farm	1.25	9.25
9.	Rue Farm to Ridge Path	1.25	10.50
10.	Ridge Path to Caundle Road	1.00	11.50
11.	Caundle Road to Stalbridge	1.00	12.50

Walking along quiet country lanes, along gently sloping Bridleways and Footpaths through small, stone-built hamlets and villages which are named in the Domesday Book, we finally arrive in Stalbridge - home of the 'Blackmore Vale Magazine' and, with no escape from learning, the seat of Robert (Boyle's Law) Boyle's father, Richard, Earl of Cork. Stalbridge High Street houses a fine market cross which dates back to the late 15th Century, behind which stands the Old Rectory. The much-quoted Hutchins (himself a Reverend) declared this to be "one of the best livings in the County". So, enjoy the Day's walk. I'll keep interrupting it with idle chat as you go on your merry way.

DAY 5 - STAGE 1

YEOVIL TO GOLF CLUB

After all too brief a sojourn in Somerset, and promising yourself to return one day for a proper visit, go back to the Old Station car park where you finished Day 4.   Leave in a North East direction along South Western Terrace, past the two bus shelters and up, past the "Alexandra" on the opposite corner.   At the top of the road, notice the old stone, probably 17th Century, "Newton Lodge" on the LH corner of Newton Road and cross over to the kissing gate in the opposite corner.   Go through the gate, signposted "Public Footpath - Sherborne Road 1/2m", past the Air-raid shelter for 50 persons, and aim for the two trees on the very top of Wyndham Hill where a quern (a Bronze-age hand-held corn ginding stone) was found.

There is a vague path which goes around the RH side of the lower slopes of the hill, against the fence, but it is frequently very muddy and rutted and it is also clear that horses use that route.   It's much fresher to go over the top.   On the other side of Wyndham Hill look down to the far RH corner of the common (ENE on the compass) and you will be able to make out a stile where the high hedge runs out.   Just aim for the stile and, just before you get there, you will join a gravel path which comes through a metal kissing gate from parallel with the railway lines.   Go up three steps where a Footpath sign points back to "Newton Road 1/2m" - very carefully, or you'll tumble straight into the very busy A30 where the traffic hurtles into and out of Yeovil.   When the opportunity presents itself, dive across the road to the security of the opposite pavement and turn right, away from the steps down to "Yeovil Pen Mill" station.   Don't be tempted to catch a train to Sherborne from here.   The Sherborne train goes from Yeovil Junction station, not here.

Keeping to the pavement, you pass the Mole Valley Suppliers on the RH side and the old Chudleigh Mill House.   The large factory on your left is Pittards, a thriving remnant of Yeovil's historic glovemaking industry.   After the LH turning to Pittard's gates, a garage and a petrol station, you arrive at the County boundary where the River Yeo flows under the A30.   The stone house with the projecting bay on the LH side after the bridge was built as a toll house, the windows facing up and down the road giving the toll-collector a good view of approaching wagons and horses.   Cross back over the A30, before the traffic island with the Dorset sign planted on it, onto the reappearing pavement and go past the "Welcome to Yeovil" sign.   The first drive on your right, after the lawn and riverside willows, on the RH side of a large DIY warehouse, leads to Yeovil Golf Club.   Don't go up this way.   Instead, keep to the proposed industrial estate road (which may or may not have been developed when you arrive) past the front of the warehouse and follow it for 1/4 mile.

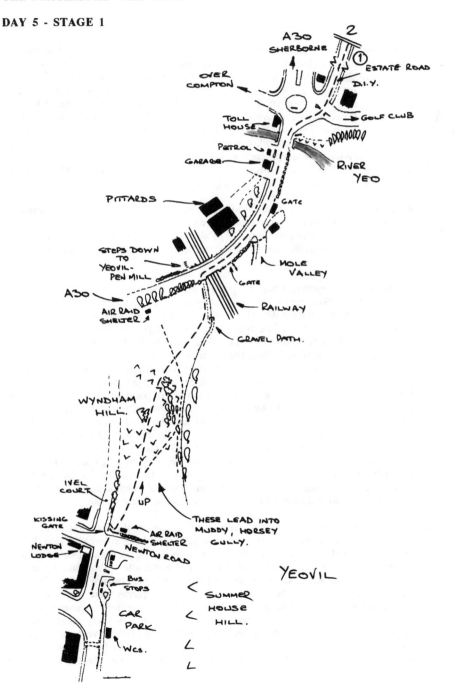

DAY 5 - STAGE 2

GOLF CLUB TO ROMAN KILNS

Past the island at the end of the estate road, you will arrive at a deeply cut hollow-way, known as Bradford Hollow - designated by Dorset County Council as an "unpaved, unmetalled, County road" - which continues in a straight line, up and away through the woods - but you won't see much of the woods because this is the deepest hollow-way you'll ever see.   To be honest, it's more like Cheddar Gorge, except that the walls are of Yeovil sands instead of limestone.   This area between Yeovil and Sherborne is Upper Lias and the rocks are of inferior oolite with doggers (rounded, sandy, ironstone blocks) protruding from the vertical faces but I'm sure you knew that already.   Anyway, the steep, shady gorge has vertical sides for half of its length, cut to ease the gradient for carts and horses.   You will have noticed that its direction backwards leads straight to the Yeo bridge entry into Yeovil

Keep on for about 200 yards to the top, passing weird tree roots and small caves on the way, and you then emerge at a junction with another ancient road, known as Leaze Lane, which comes from your right.   The all-forbidding notice on the gate which you pass on your way onto the lane refers only to Leaze Lane, definitely not to our route - I've checked with County Hall.

On the lane, turn right and begin a gradual descent with, at first, a cut rock face on your right and banked trees an your left.   As you descend, a gate leads behind the trees on your left and a lane turns down to your right.   There are several right turns before the one which you want, so just keep straight on for now, following the Stage Map and enjoying the views across Blackmore Vale on your right.   There are wide verges from time to time along here for refuge in time of need so settle down for an easy 1 mile stroll.   On the way, after a confined section with no verges, you pass a fine stone house called "Coombe" with a walled garden and a turning to "Over Compton 1.1/4" on the left.   This lane leads to the highest point of Babylon Hill where, during the Civil War which broke out in 1642, a great battle took place between the King's forces under the Marquis of Hertford and the rebel forces under the Earl of Bedford.   Hertford's forces were stationed at Sherborne Castle where they were besieged by Bedford's army but 'after several indecisive skirmishes' Bedford's army retired to Yeovil.   Later, Hertford's army was reported to be gathering on Babylon Hill with the intention of entering Yeovil by way of the Yeo Bridge but, on hearing of this, Bedford's forces attacked them and the Battle of Babylon Hill followed.   The Royalist forces were defeated and they retreated to Sherborne Castle.

After this crossing, with a row of tall pine trees leading the way down to Bradford Abbas, keep straight on up the steeper, unverged lane where, after a gate into the field on your right and a pair of gates into a concrete barn yard, the higher field on your left is the site of the 1877 excavation of East Farm Roman site.   Professor J Buckman, owner of the farm, found several pieces of pottery and small broken querns (hand held corn grinding stones) in the 50 acre field.   These querns were made of Cornish granite and volcanic gritstone from the Rhine and the excavation uncovered five kiln firing pits in surrounding stone-paved floors.   These separately sited kilns were most likely used for corn drying but, unfortunately, the sites have been covered by modern cornfields and no Roman villa or settlement has been found up here.   However, a Roman villa was unearthed a mile South from here - on the other side of the River Yeo.

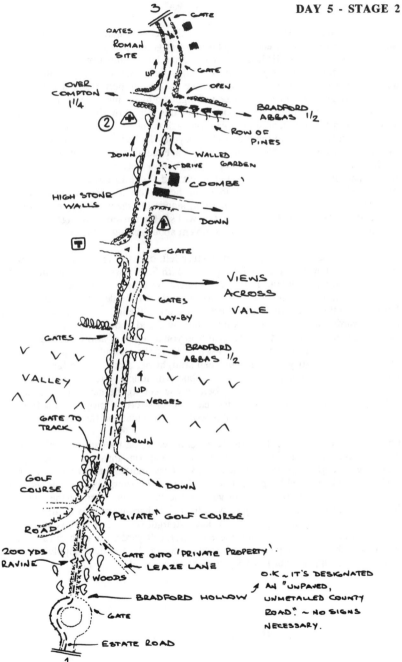

GATE

GATES
ROMAN
SITE

UP

GATE

OPEN

OVER
COMPTON
1¼

BRADFORD
ABBAS ½

ROW OF
PINES

② ✚

DOWN

WALLED
DRIVE GARDEN

'COOMBE'

HIGH STONE
WALLS

DOWN

⚠️

🅃

GATE

VIEWS
ACROSS
VALE

GATES

LAY-BY

GATES

BRADFORD
ABBAS ½

VALLEY

UP

VERGES

DOWN

GATE TO
TRACK

DOWN

GOLF
COURSE

"PRIVATE" GOLF COURSE

ROAD

GATE ONTO 'PRIVATE PROPERTY'.

200 YDS
RAVINE

LEAZE LANE

O.K ~ IT'S DESIGNATED
AN "UNPAVED,
UNMETALLED COUNTY
ROAD". ~ NO SIGNS
NECESSARY.

WOODS

BRADFORD HOLLOW

GATE

ESTATE ROAD

DAY 5 - STAGE 3

ROMAN KILNS TO SILVERLAKE FARM

As you pass under the H.V. overhead wires, the verge is quite wide on the right with fine views across the Vale and, as you descend slightly, past a LH gate in the banked hedge and an oak in the RH hedge, you arrive at a kerbed junction with a lane coming in from your right. The signpost on the grass verge shows that you are practically mid-way between Yeovil and Sherborne but the finger pointing down the merging lane will probably be missing. Keep straight on again but, after a few more yards, opposite two gates and a brick cottage on the left, turn right and begin an easy descent down the side lane with a gate on each corner. The verges on both sides soon run out whilst, up in the high fields, beyond the hedges on either side, there are two rows of sycamores which form a perfect avenue all the way down this lane - and it's fully 1/2 a mile to the end. Keep on down, now becoming steep sided, until you reach a pair of red-brick cottages on your left and Wyke Cottage on your right. Go past the RH turning and you will arrive in the Wyke Farm area of tracks, low stone walls and paddocks. Over on your right, stands the magnificent long, stone Tithe Barn and past the LH end of the barn, you will see the railway crossing. There is also a bridge over our lane, so there is no problem about getting to the other side.

However, we need to stay on this side so turn left, over the stile with the yellow arrow in the wooden fence next to the farm gate. With fine views across the line and fields to the wooded ridge on your right, walk straight across this level field to the strip of sycamore, ash, willow and elderberry woods on the other side. There is a much wider field on the other side with a high beech hedge up on the left. Before starting across this 300 yards wide field, choose a line which will end about 20 yards to the right of the cottage on the other side. This will lead you to a pair of arrow-marked stiles with a deep ditch in the mixed trees in-between. Over the second stile, join a farm track which goes down to your right but keep straight on, along the hedge of the stone cottage on your left and past a gate in the short wire fence. Around the LH corner, go over the RH stile in the wire fence before you get to the gate which leads to the cottage. Now, you're in for a nice, easy, level stroll on properly cut field edges through farmland for about 1.1/2 miles so enjoy the quiet and the pastoral scenery.

On a good, grass track, follow the fence and hedge, past a cattle trough and with a mixed wood across the field on your right. Keep on, through an opening in the facing fence and hedge into the next field. Pass another trough on your right and keep to the winding LH hedge, then fence, then a LH opening and a small beech wood, until you reach a conglomeration of gates in the far corner. Ignore the gates on the left and go through the smaller gate with the painted arrow, next to a farm gate in the wire fence across your route and still keep straight on. The path is still wide and grassy with a beech hedge alongside but, after 100 yards, the path goes straight on between the hedge and a patch of old weeds. Suddenly, the field doubles in width as your hedge disappears but just keep straight on across it.

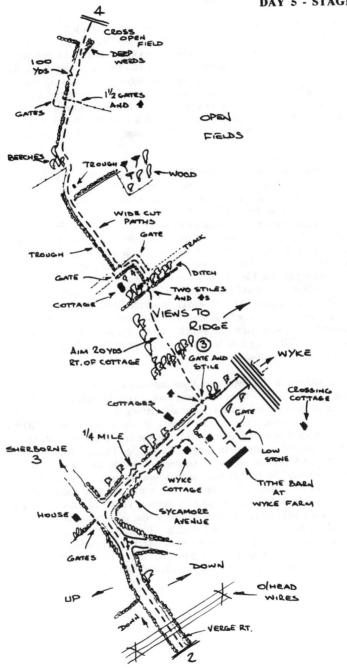

4

CROSS OPEN FIELD

DEEP WEEDS

100 YDS

1½ GATES AND ↑

GATES

OPEN FIELDS

BEECHES

TROUGH

WOOD

WIDE CUT PATHS

GATE

TROUGH

TRACK

GATE

DITCH

COTTAGE

TWO STILES AND ↑s

VIEWS TO RIDGE

AIM 20 YDS RT. OF COTTAGE

③

GATE AND STILE

WYKE

CROSSING COTTAGE

COTTAGES

GATE

¼ MILE

LOW STONE

SHERBORNE 3

WYKE COTTAGE

TITHE BARN AT WYKE FARM

HOUSE

SYCAMORE AVENUE

GATES

DOWN

UP

O/HEAD WIRES

DOWN

VERGE RT.

2

97

DAY 5 - STAGE 4

SILVERLAKE FARM TO LENTHAY ROAD

At first, aim to the right of the last, RH slate roofed barn and, half-way across the field, you will see a stile in the facing fence. Go over the fence and across a short, grassy section to the next stile by a short wooden fence. As you go over this stile with the painted arrow, notice the stone wall and the very deep, wide ditch which go off into the dense trees and bushes on your right. Then, with the lovely, stone, climber-clad Silverlake Farm house over on your left, go up the initial slope of this field until you see that this is a particularly vast field spread out in front of you. Facing you, there is a banked, wire fence which joins the fence beyond the farmhouse but the facing fence soon turns away and continues ahead of you towards the far end of the field.

Aim for the corner where this fence turns away (this is on a slightly right bearing for you) and, as you stroll towards it, you will meet a weaving path which comes from a stile near the farmhouse and heads across this field towards its far RH corner, all of 1/4 mile away. Join this path as it wends its inebriated way across towards the far corner, meeting the scrubby-bushed wire fence of a smaller field on your right before you reach a stile in the corner. Go over this stile in the wire fence and instantly turn left into a long, triangular shaped grassy area with a grass track coming down towards you from the far end. This is a short section of Bridleway, the first today, and you follow it alongside the LH wire fence to a low, scrubby hummock before a complex of gates and stiles in the top LH corner. (The first LH stile and gate come in from the field that you have just left). However, leave the Bridleway and turn right around the bush on top of the hummock, aiming for the lower, shrub-filled corner on the right. Go through the iron kissing gate which is in the corner and turn right into the field on the other side, following a wide, grassy path next to the RH hedge of elderberries and hawthorns - then sycamores.

At the far RH end of this last field, your pastoral idyll is over for a while as you are coming into Sherborne - from the newer end. But the old, medieval town is reputed to be one of the most beautiful in England, having the air of a small cathedral city so it's well worth a visit. Go over the stile, with bungalows over the RH fence and new houses over the fence on your left. Follow the enclosed path to its hedged end where you meet the first of the estate roads, Westbridge Park. Cross over into the next passageway, with No.26 on its LH corner, and let the assorted wood and wire fences guide you around the far left bend onto South Avenue. Again, cross over and go straight on into a short cul-de-sac with a turning circle at the other end. Keeping straight on, follow the footpath past the turning circle and, still between houses, you arrive in a derelict playground area. Follow the path anti-clockwise into the far RH corner where another path leaves the area. Continue between garden hedges, past a central post, into the avenue of small trees which line Lenthay Road. Turn left onto Lenthay Road with estate houses still on your left at first and with 'Springfield' and a gate onto Sherborne School Playing Fields on your right.

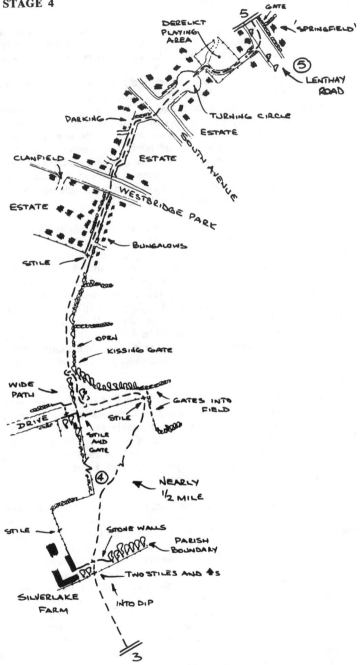

DAY 5 - STAGE 5

LENTHAY ROAD TO SHERBORNE

From here, it's a straight road all the way into Sherborne old town so, apart from pointing out a few areas and road names on your way, I'll leave you to make your way there with the minimum of interruption.   Have a good look around on the way.

Passing Lenthay Close and the cemetery on your left, you still have the playing fields over the hedge on your right and, at the traffic lights at the end of Lenthay Road, there are a couple of long rows of cottages,.   Use the pedestrian crossing over Horsecastles Lane and keep straight on past "Skippers" Inn on the LH corner, onto the raised pavement on the LH side of Horsecastles.   The high stone wall opposite shelters the tennis courts and the cricket pitches of Sherborne School and a fine clock-towered pavilion.   Keep on, past a LH turning with a telephone box up on the left, past Richmond Road, and on to cross Acreman Street into Trendle Street.   At the end of Trendle Street, join Half Moon Street from your right as you come to the magnificent, mellow-stone structure of Sherborne Abbey.

Now you can have a rest whilst I tell you something about Sherborne.   It appears in the Domesday Book as *Scireburne*, from the Saxon for 'clear stream' under the ownership of the Bishop of Salisbury, formerly Queen Edith's.   Ina, king of the Saxons founded a monastery and an episcopal See here in 705 AD.   Benedictine rule was introduced to the monastery in 998 AD and the Benedictine quest for learning somehow spread into modern Sherborne which boasts ten schools, two of national renown.   The Saxon See was removed to Old Sarum in 1075 but the Sarum Bishops kept the office of Abbot of Sherborne until the time of Roger of Caen who separated these two offices.   He appointed Thurstan to be Abbot of Sherborne and, at the same time, had the old church demolished, replacing it with a much larger, finer church of Norman design.   There is so much to see in the Abbey that I would recommend a fuller visit and the purchase of an official guide.

Before you leave, though, look at the corner of Half Moon Street and Trendle Street where you arrived and you will see the still used Almshouse of St John the Baptist and St John the Evangelist which was founded as a hospital of the Order of St Augustin on 20th January 1448 by Robert Neville, Bishop of Sarum.   Throughout the old town, there are 17th, 18th and 19th Century houses all crammed into intriguing, narrow streets but it's time to leave for now.   Promise yourself a return to this lovely town - It's a great place to spend a day or a weekend or even longer.

With your back to the South transept (or front steps) of the Abbey, the street ahead of you is Digby Street.   That's right - the Digbys of Minterne Magna who have also owned Sherborne 'New' Castle since 1617.   Now, go down Digby Street, calling in at the Tourist Information Office on the right and passing Digby Hall and the Day Centre on the left.   Go past the Conveniences on the right, before the garage and opposite the Police Station and Magistrates' Court, then either continue along Digby Street to Sherborne Railway Station at the end or divert through the park gate immediately after the Courts.   Either way, follow the sign for "Riverside Walk to Old Castle 1/2" which stands outside the far gates of the park.   Cross over to the Station and follow the pavement round, past the platform gate and the telephone boxes, to go over the railway crossing by the signal box into Gas House Hill.   Keep to the RH pavement, past 'Hillside' and note the views on your left to the ruins of Sherborne Old Castle as you begin to go up the hill.

THE BLACKMORE VALE PATH

DAY 5 - STAGE 5

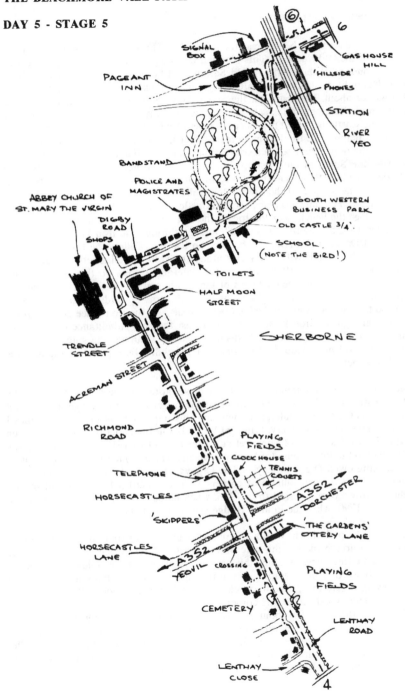

SIGNAL BOX

GAS HOUSE HILL

'HILLSIDE'

PAGEANT INN

PHONES

STATION

RIVER YEO

BANDSTAND

POLICE AND MAGISTRATES

ABBEY CHURCH OF ST. MARY THE VIRGIN

SOUTH WESTERN BUSINESS PARK

DIGBY ROAD

'OLD CASTLE 3/4'.

SHOPS

SCHOOL (NOTE THE BIRD!)

TOILETS

HALF MOON STREET

SHERBORNE

TRENDLE STREET

ACREMAN STREET

RICHMOND ROAD

PLAYING FIELDS

CLOCK HOUSE

TELEPHONE

TENNIS COURTS

HORSECASTLES

A352 DORCHESTER

'SKIPPERS'

'THE GARDENS' OTTERY LANE

HORSECASTLES LANE

A352

YEOVIL CROSSING

PLAYING FIELDS

CEMETERY

LENTHAY ROAD

LENTHAY CLOSE

4

101

DAY 5 - STAGE 6

SHERBORNE TO SHERBORNE PARK

Have a short rest on the bench near the top of Gas House Hill whilst you find out something of the Old Castle. This Norman building was built by Bishop Roger of Salisbury, builder of the castle at Old Sarum, and both are actually more fortified palaces than military structures. After Roger fell from power, the Castle was held by the Crown for about 200 years but the Salisbury bishops regained it in 1354. The dissolution of the monasteries saw the demise of many ecclesiastical properties so, by 1591, the Castle belonged to Queen Elizabeth I who granted it, and the manor, to Sir Walter Raleigh. He tried to modernise it but it was far too uncomfortable so he abandoned the project and began a conversion of an early Tudor hunting lodge which stood 1/4 mile South in the existing deer park. This building eventually became Sherborne 'New' Castle which we will see in a few minutes time. During the Civil Wars, Sherborne supported the king, (Remember the Battle of Babylon Hill?) and after two sieges, Parliament ordered the Old Castle's complete destruction. Now, let's press on. Past the bench near the top of the hill, cross over the main road, signed "Dorchester A352 and Shaftesbury A30", and go through the iron kissing gate onto the slopes of Dancing Hill (Dogs to be kept on lead). Follow the faint grass track along and up the hillside with fine views along the valley to Sherborne Castle - this was the one which was built by Sir Walter Raleigh in 1594 so this is the "new" Castle. There are much better views of the Castle and Capability Brown's lake as you progress up and past the hill and, as the path turns upwards, notice the Castle Lodge and the entrance gates to the Park below you. As the iron fence comes up the slope, go through the iron kissing gate, just past the "No Admittance to Castle or Grounds" sign and a couple of hawthorns near the top. Through the gate, look down and across the 1/4 mile wide field beyond and you will a faint path heading towards the far LH corner.

Before you go, this is a suitable spot for a dissertation on Sherborne New Castle. Built on a limestone knoll which supported the original hunting lodge, the central section of this Castle was Raleigh's home until his imprisonment in 1603. James I gave the Castle to his son Henry, Prince of Wales but he died after two years. It then passed to Robert Carr, Earl of Somerset but, after his fall in 1617, James granted the whole estate to Sir John Digby (of Minterne Magna on Day 4) for a knock-down price - but the King owed Digby money. The Digbys added the four wings and the low hexagonal towers at their outermost corners. The beautiful Park was laid out by Capability Brown over a period from 1756, when he dammed the stream to form the huge lake, to 1790, when the Pinfold Bridge was built at its head.

Now, follow the path down, with a vast wood over on your right and, after the old, bare oak, go through the kissing gate onto the estate track which comes from your left. There are fine views all along this path and track across the fields to Sherborne Castle - well worth a photograph. From the gate, follow the track around its LH bend, passing a gate to a 'Private' track in the RH corner, a Footpath sign on the fence and a small wood on the LH corner. Now, on a level track with grass up the middle, enjoy the stroll for about 1/2 mile. through another kissing gate next to a farm gate and up the track to another kissing gate. There is a fenced wood on your right and the high wire fence on your left is to keep the deer inside their park. The park contains a mix of mostly old ash and sycamore trees whilst there is a single, huge oak on the steep RH slope after the wood. Keep straight on, on the gravel track.

DAY 5 - STAGE 6

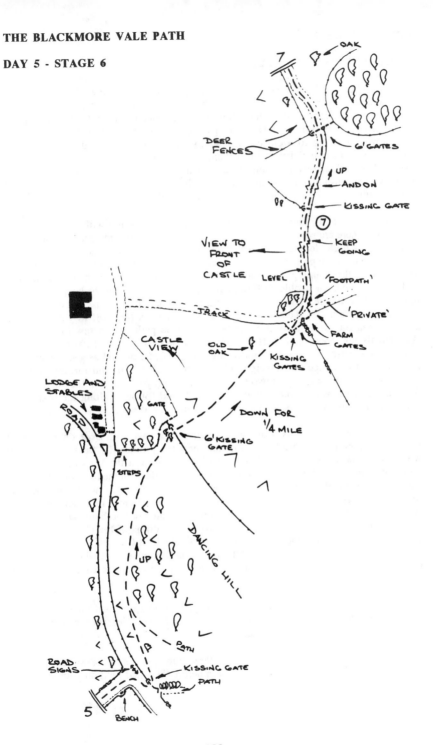

DAY 5 - STAGE 7

SHERBORNE PARK TO HAYDON

Go through the next high wooden kissing gate onto a tarmac drive which passes the old, thatched hunting lodge on your right.   Hunting was strictly by special invitation of the Digbys but, with the fallow deer population down to 280 during the patronage of F J B Wingfield-Digby Esq in the 1860s, the days of hunting parties were slowly drawing to a close.   After the iron-fenced lodge, go up the steep, bracken-covered slope of Jerusalem Hill and cross the level top on the gravel track to another Footpath-arrowed kissing gate into a mixed, pine and deciduous wood. Before you go through the gate though, have a look behind you, beyond the parkland trees, for fine views over the lowlands towards Yeovil.

During World War II, there was an American Military hospital within these woods. That is why there are several concrete bases and tracks in the undergrowth and that is why there is a high, derelict brick water tower over on your right just after you enter the woods but, although there have been several books written about Dorset's part in World War II, the planning and launching of the D-Day assault from its beaches and harbours, I have been unable to find anything about this extensive hospital base or those who served here.   So, follow the path as it winds through the woods to a wire fence on your right.   At the end of the fence, a larger track turns off to your right but keep straight on, along a solid concrete and tarmac path with a few branches off. With mostly pine trees on the RH side and mixed woods on the left, you soon arrive in a tarmac clearing with a plethora of high corrugated iron and asbestos buildings, together with an office and a weighbridge.   Ignore all tracks and turnings off and follow the main drive out, past two Footpath arrows on your right on the way.   Join the main driveway which comes up from your left and follow it along the high slope with fine views across the park to valleys and woods on your left.

Carry on along the drive, past an ancient oak with a vast girth over on your right before a remaining WW2 brick building, and past the joining RH track before small woods on either side which straddle the driveway.   Go past the Victorian Sherborne Park lodge and through the ornate black iron gates (or through the heavy iron kissing gate) and aim straight across the verge - down the entrance drive - and across the road to the lane to the left of the little church.   Haydon church, in Dean Chandler's Register, is said to be "a chapel, dependent on the Church of Sherborne and is founded in honour of St Katherine".   The Digbys have been patrons of the church since they gained the manor from Thomas Chafe Esq in the late 17th Century.   Nothing much seems to change around here - In 1801, there was a population of 83 and, by 1901, this had changed to 89.   I don't suppose there has been much increase, if any, since then.

There is a Footpath running from about 100 yards down the road on your left and across the fields, nearly to Rue Farm, but it's a much easier, pleasant stroll down this lane past Haydon Farmhouse instead.

So follow the lane past the church with its three huge pines and the walled cemetery on the right, and down past a fine, stone barn before the gated field on your left.

THE BLACKMORE VALE PATH

DAY 5 - STAGE 7

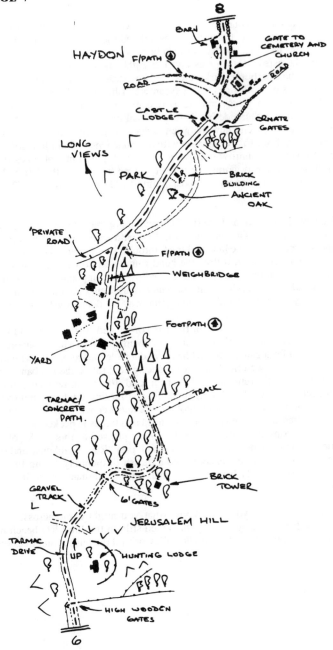

DAY 5 - STAGE 8

HAYDON TO RUE FARM

Past "Haydon Farmhouse" on the RH side and stone-walled barns and outbuildings on both sides of the lane, the tarmac runs out and the narrower, rough and winding gravel track begins to ascend between beech hedges. At the left bend at the top of the rise, through the pair of farm gates on your right, there is a fine view back over the low valley to the Sherborne Park gates. Now, keep going as the track levels out, past several gates on both sides and a sycamore, ash, oak and beech wood on the LH side. The track gains a grassy middle as it begins a gentle descent between high hedges with a ditch on either side but, before a small mixed wood on the left, the ditches have gone again. Descend now, between hedges thick with bracken and travellers' joy in the summer, down to a T-junction with a tarmac lane. Turn left, still between hedges, almost level now, until you arrive at another T-junction - of lanes this time with an additional Bridleway going off between close hedges on the left and a farm gate on each corner. The County signpost points to "Purse Caundle 1.1/2" straight on and this is our route.

Follow the lane down and, on the RH bend, a Footpath arrow points through the gate in the LH corner. This is where the Footpath from the lane by the Sherborne Park lodge re-emerges. The lane and track through Haydon and the lane down to here were much easier. Anyway, follow the bend round and down to where it sweeps round to the left. At the junction with the ascending lane opposite, go past the farm gate in the RH hedge and another signpost which maintains that Purse Caundle is still 1.1/2 miles away. Lucky we're not going that way - it doesn't get any nearer.

So, go past the brick house on the LH corner and begin to ascend the verged lane, between hedges and with a covering of overhead oaks and sycamores. At the first bend, with a farm gate in the RH hedge and a wider space on the left with a few trees in front of a wire-fenced field and an entrance gate, I sat on the LH bank for a quick coffee and, whilst quietly ruminating, I heard a loud drumming noise coming from the trees on the left. I stayed as still as possible, just turning my head, and was rewarded with the sight of a beautiful greater spotted woodpecker with its distinguishing black and white patches and red flashes from its head and tail as it pecked at tree trunk after tree trunk in its constant search for food. Very pleased at this stroke of good fortune, I carried on up the lane (as you must do) and, past "Rue" farmhouse and the collection of barns on the right, I next encountered a thrush desperately trying to open his packed lunch. It was noisily hammering a snail onto the tarmac - right in the middle of the road.

So, tread quietly and you never know what you might come across. However, keep on up the lane, passing a Footpath-signed stile in the high RH beech hedge and with quite a drop into the Purse Caundle valley behind the bushes and trees on the LH side.

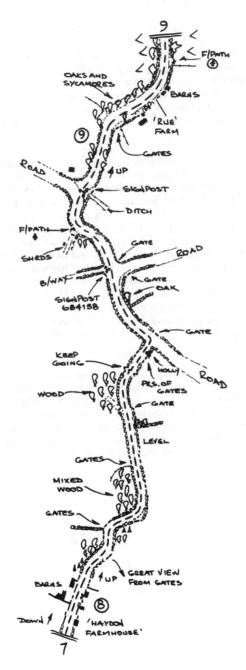

DAY 5 - STAGE 9

RUE FARM TO RIDGE PATH

On along the level lane, past a Footpath-signed gate on the right and a half-gate on the left, you reach Plumley Wood dropping away on the LH side whilst the fields on the right are quite highly banked. The lane is quite level now as you pass the turning to Woodrow Farm and its buildings on your right and ranks of chicken sheds on your left. The Bridleway, signed at the entrance to the sheds, leads down to Purse Caundle. However, keep straight on, past another Footpath-arrowed stile in the LH beech hedge and past a few modern bungalows, a paddock and an orchard, until you reach the last brick house with staddle-stones on its verge at the RH corner of a T-junction.

After the house, there is a Footpath arrow post next to the gate into the RH corner field but ignore it. Turn right, down the lane for about 50 yards until, with farm gates on either side and another one facing you, two Bridleway arrows (one on a post and one on the LH gates post) indicate your route into the LH field. Follow the fenced edge of the mixed wood on the right of this level field until you come to a single, small oak in the field, not far from the edge of the wood. If the field is fallow, aim for the half-gate in the hedge, about 30 yards from the RH corner, but, if it is planted, keep following the wood and turn left in the far RH corner to get to this gate. The gate has both a Footpath arrow and a Bridleway arrow - both pointing in different directions. In this high, level field with fine views ahead and over to the right, follow the Bridleway direction, along the LH hedge until you come to a gate. Go through the gate and turn instantly right to follow the same hedge but on its other side. The fields slope gently away on your left to show a chequered pattern of hedges across the low valley whilst the top fields of this low ridge continue over the hedge on your right.

Keep following the hedge, going through another gate and passing gates into the top RH field, until you reach a facing hedge where a half-gate with a Bridleway arrow on it stands near its RH corner. Go through the gate and bear slightly left to a gap in the LH hedge, not far from the near corner. There is a confirmation Bridleway arrow on a post and there is a ditch on the other side of the hedge as you join a wide, cut track across the next, downward-sloping field. The large house across the fields, ahead and to your left, is Manor Farm, Stalbridge Weston.

THE BLACKMORE VALE PATH

DAY 5 - STAGE 9

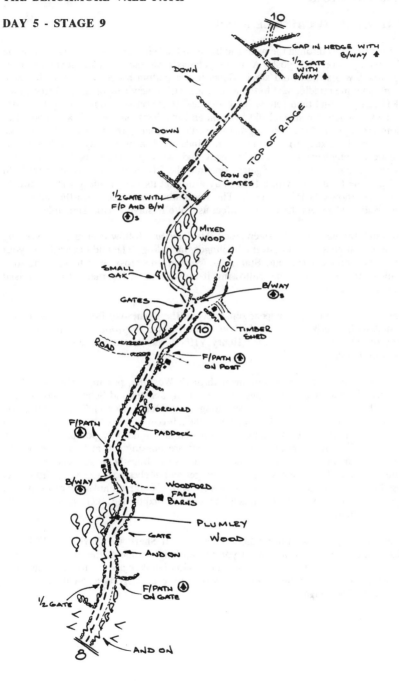

RIDGE PATH TO CAUNDLE ROAD

Down the field, go through the wide gap between the hedge and the wire fence with the Bridleway arrow on a RH post. A similar gap leads into the LH field, next to a small mixed wood, whilst this field slopes down to the bottom hedge. Follow the track with grass up the middle, next to the wire fence with a new row of planted trees, past the RH end gate and then follow the hedge and fence on your right to a gate across your track. There are several old trees on an earth bank on your LH side and, after passing through the Bridleway-signed gate into a wider grazing area with the trees still on your left, keep to the track as it winds its downward way in a low gully. There are scrubby hawthorns in the RH bank and, when you reach the bottom of this field, there is a set of three farm gates - one into the RH field, one into the next field ahead and the final one, with a Bridleway arrow on its post, leading onto a rough, stony track known as Pile Lane. The Footpaths around here are the subject of reorganisation plans but these won't affect us. We're staying with the Bridleway.

Go through the gate into the steep-sided Pile Lane and follow it around a sweeping bend until you pass the stone-walled cottages, including "The Old Orchard" on your right. You now emerge into Stalbridge Weston and cross over to the flagstone pavement on the facing side, following it around the RH corner with the raised pavement opposite.

Stalbridge Weston doesn't appear separately in the Domesday Book because it was included with Sherborne - "the bishop himself holds *Westone*" and, in the 1535 survey of religious properties for Henry VIII, it was listed as belonging to the Sherborne monks.

Follow the lane of ribbon development through *Westone*, passing "The Old Dairy House" and its associated buildings (all converted) and the old School House on the right, with Corner Farm a little further along on the left. Descending slightly, you arrive at a T-junction where a bus-shelter on the left corner has a "Weston" sign fixed to it. A damaged County signpost on the central island only points to "Stourton Caundle 1.1/4" to the right since all other arms are missing (or, at least, they were). Ignore the narrow lane opposite and turn left to follow the wide, level and easy Stourton Caundle to Stalbridge lane, with verges and ditches both sides. A little way along the road, there is a farm gate and a stile with a Footpath arrow over in the left hedge and, as you drop down towards a low, stone walled bridge, there is another gate into the RH field.

I haven't given you much information since you left Sherborne, have I? Still, it's probably nice to be left alone whilst you are walking - some of the time. I'll bore you some more on Stage 11 when you get to Stalbridge Park and the town which holds the Blackmore Vale ethralled every Thursday with each, eagerly awaited issue of the "Blackmore Vale Magazine".

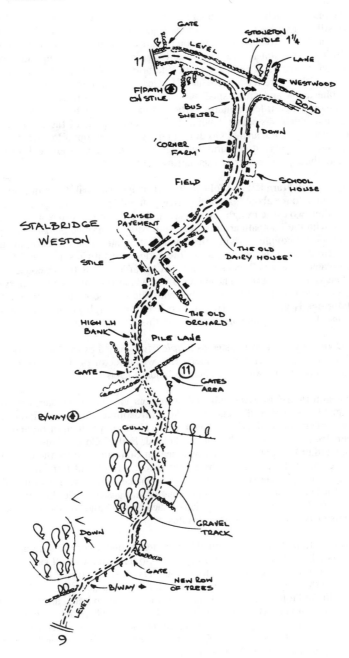

CAUNDLE ROAD TO STALBRIDGE

Over the bridge which carries a small stream on its way to join the River Lydden, go past the stile with a Footpath arrow in the right hedge and up to another T-junction of lanes.   The high, stone wall facing you is part of the five miles long boundary wall of Stalbridge Mansion House - now, sadly, no more.   Go through the gate in the wall, finger posted as "Public Footpath. Stalbridge 3/4", and across the field on the other side with a wire fence on your RH side.   Go through two gates, each with a painted blue arrow and with a small wood over the fence between them.   The hedge which is now on your left contains vertical stone slabs which probably came from the old mansion which was pulled down in 1822.   Other parts of the old house were re-used extensively in the area.   Go through the gate at the top of this field into a long, narrow field with large stone barns away on your left.   Turn right and walk across to the gate in the top LH corner of this narrow field.

Through the gate, turn left and follow the LH hedge with oak trees interspersed in it, up the steep field for about 200 yards when you will pass a large single oak on your right.   After two cattle troughs and a gate in the LH hedge, keep straight on up to the next gate with the Footpath arrow across your path.   Through the gate, keep straight on again, past a couple of dying trees and past a gate to an old barn, in the top LH corner.   Go through the facing gate in the hedge and turn instantly right, before the single sycamore, as a path goes slightly left towards the 1870 farmhouse where once stood The Mansion House.   The church tower which you can see is St Mary's Church which also stands in the old grounds but which is now accessible from the far end of the Stalbridge High Street.   Before you leave this high ground and descend into Stalbridge, let me tell you something about this ancient town:

In the Domesday Book, it is listed as *Staplebrige*, owned by the Bishop of Salisbury. John Barnstaple, once Abbot of Sherborne, was a rector of the   Perpendicular style Church of St Mary and was buried here in January 1560.

The Mansion House, as was mentioned during our visit to Yetminster, was once home to the great scientist and founder of the Philosophical Society (later the Royal Society) Robert Boyle of Boyle's Law fame.   He, too, was born in Ireland - Lismore, 25th Feb 1627.   He was the 7th son of Richard, Earl of Cork.   During his studies at Eton, his father brought him to his own seat at Stalbridge under the care of William Douch, rector of the parish.   His father died in 1643 and left him the manor of Stalbridge where Boyle stayed until 1650 when he moved to London amidst great acclaim for his scientific work with pneumatics and gases.   He died 30th Dec 1691. The Mansion House was eventually demolished in 1822 and, in 1854, the Marquis of Westminster bought the Stalbridge Estates.

Now, having turned right, carry on along the RH hedge, over the stile and across the small wooded area to a corrugated iron gate.   Go through the small gate and turn right onto the pavement alongside the stone boundary wall.   Follow the pavement, past the gates to the Playing Fields and on to the T-junction at its end.   Turn left, onto Barrow Hill, and follow the LH pavement all the way down until, after the junction of streets shown on your Map, you arrive in Stalbridge.   There are several Inns, a Post Office on the corner of High Street and an excellent bus service.   Have a rest after an excellent Day's walking and we'll find out more about Stalbridge on Day 6 before we set out for journey's end at Blandford Forum.

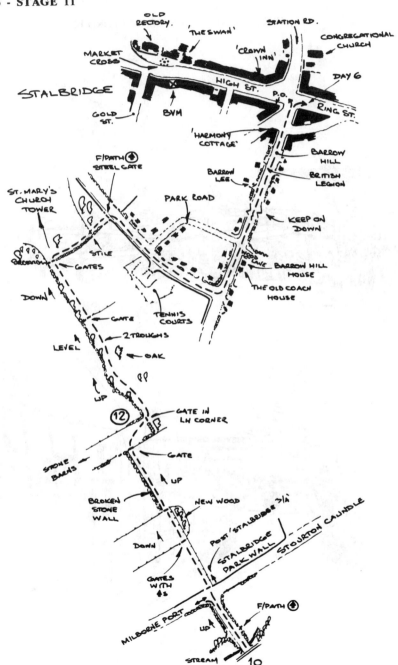

STALBRIDGE

OLD RECTORY.

'THE SWAN'

STATION RD.

'CROWN INN'

CONGREGATIONAL CHURCH

MARKET CROSS

HIGH ST.

DAY 6

P.O.

RING ST.

GOLD ST.

BVM

'HARMONY COTTAGE'

BARROW HILL

BRITISH LEGION

BARROW LEE

F/PATH ⊕
STEEL GATE

PARK ROAD

KEEP ON DOWN

ST. MARY'S CHURCH TOWER

STILE

GATES

LANE

BARROW HILL HOUSE

THE OLD COACH HOUSE

DOWN

GATE

TENNIS COURTS

2 TROUGHS

LEVEL

OAK

UP

⑫

GATE IN LH CORNER

GATE

STONE BARNS

UP

BROKEN STONE WALL

NEW WOOD

Post 'STALBRIDGE 3/4'

STALBRIDGE PARK WALL

STOURTON CAUNDLE

DOWN

GATES WITH 4s

MILBORNE PORT

UP

F/PATH ⊕

STREAM

10

113

THE BLACKMORE VALE PATH

TOP: COLBER BRIDGE, STURMINSTER NEWTON - PAGE 122

BOTTOM: ST. ANDREW'S, OKEFORD FITZPAINE - PAGE 130

DAY 6 - INTRODUCTION

STALBRIDGE TO BLANDFORD FORUM

The last Day - and I for one will be very sad to finish this Path.   I feel as if I've seen so much of the 'real' Dorset in the last 5 Days that the completion of The Blackmore Vale Path will be an occasion for a little sadness - but what memories we shall all have after this journey.   Today, we leave Stalbridge (more details on Stage 1) on an easy lane and, on our route today, we cross several streams and the River Lydden en route for the River Stour.   We cross the Stour itself when we get to the market town of Sturminster Newton - the other claimant for the title of "capital of Blackmore Vale'.   There are associations with William Barnes, Thomas Hardy and the painter Hogarth during this walk as we join ancient hollow-ways and pass several chapels left over from the fervent days of Wesley and the Primitive Methodists.   The route goes through just one village of any size today whilst three others - Bagber, Colmer and Angiers - have disappeared due to decay or fire.

You can look forward to a visit to a lovely village church which was restored by Thomas Hardy's first employer and to tramping up and over Okeford Hill.   Very fittingly for the last Day, the views over Blackmore Vale are superlative and retrospective, giving plenty of opportunity for looking back, figuratively and metaphorically, over the glorious few days you have spent in the company of some of the most beautiful villages, farms and countryside in all England.

	STAGE	MILES	TOTAL MILES
1.	Stalbridge to Bibberne Farm	1.00	1.00
2.	Bibberne Farm to Bagber	1.25	2.25
3.	Bagber to Mill Lane	1.00	3.25
4.	Mill Lane to Sturminster Newton	0.75	4.00
5.	Sturminster Newton to Broad Oak Path	1.00	5.00
6.	Broad Oak Path to Okeford Hollow-way	1.00	6.00
7.	Okeford Hollow-way to Okeford Fitzpaine	1.00	7.00
8.	Okeford Fitzpaine to Okeford Hill	1.00	8.00
9.	Okeford Hill to Bonsley Common	1.25	9.25
10.	Bonsley Common to Field Grove	1.00	10.25
11.	Field Grove to Shothole	0.75	11.00
12.	Shothole to Beech Clump	1.25	12.25
13.	Beech Clump to Blandford Forum	1.00	13.25

DAY 6 - STAGE 1

STALBRIDGE TO BIBBERNE FARM

Before you leave Stalbridge, I really think you should wander up the High Street and have a look at the 14th Century market cross.   It's quite remarkable how it has survived so long, especially the last 20 years with the ever-present threat from the huge lorries which pass only feet away from it.   Behind the cross, stands The Old Rectory - of which Hutchins wrote "it is one of the best livings in Dorset".   The offices of the famous Blackmore Vale Magazine are on the opposite side of the High Street.   The new issues are published on Thursdays and I would recommend that you get hold of a copy - it really must be the best informed and most brilliantly presented free local newspaper/magazine in the whole country.

Stalbridge's growth was based upon the manufacture of stockings (Malvolio wore yellow stockings, cross gartered, in Shakespeare's 'Twelfth Night' and they were the height of fashion much later throughout the Restoration years).   The stockings made in Stalbridge were reputed to be "the finest, best and highest prized in England", but the industry fell into decay in the early 19th Century "by the introduction of the knitting frame".

As there is just a little further to walk today, I thought we'd get the first three miles under our belts with an easy, level walk along quiet country lanes before we turn off for Sturminster Newton so walk back down the High Street, past the Post Office and the junction with Barrow Hill where you arrived from Day 5, and continue out of town down Ring Street.   Past Stalbridge Methodist Church and Stalbridge Close on the left, you will see Westminster Cottages after the 'phone box on the right.   The Westminster connection, I'm sure you remember, goes back to the Marquis who bought the Stalbridge Estates in 1854.   When you reach the village green, with its ornate pump, the sign to "Village Hall and Marnhull 4" and the huge lime tree at its furthest end, bear left and pass the stone mullioned cottages on the LH pavement.   It may be of passing interest that the road sign indicates "A357 Sturminster Newton 6" along the main road - but it's only 4 miles the way we're going.   So, enjoy the morning air as you continue, past the Village Hall on the left and the "Stalbridge Arms" on the right.   After Coppern Way on your left, Bartlett Close and some bungalows on your right and Lower Road on your left, notice the fine stone-walled "Sandhills" on the RH side, just before the first gate into the first field of the Day, and, when the new houses of Jarvis Way and 'Springfields' are past, you have fields behind the hedges and various verges on both sides.

Between two gates on the left, a road sign warns of "Oncoming Vehicles in Middle of Road" so, when you reach the low stone-parapetted bridge over a tributary of the River Stour, take care.   A Footpath-arrowed path comes out over a stile from the field on your left just after the LH parapet and joins our route after a confirmation arrowed marker post.   The very smart, tree-filled lawns opposite lead to Bibberne Farm and the wide verge past here may come in handy as a refuge from time to time.   When you reach the cross-roads on Stage 2, most of the cars turn left for Marnhull or right for Sturminster Newton and the next stretch of lane is much quieter, so just keep strolling on - you've walked 1 mile already.

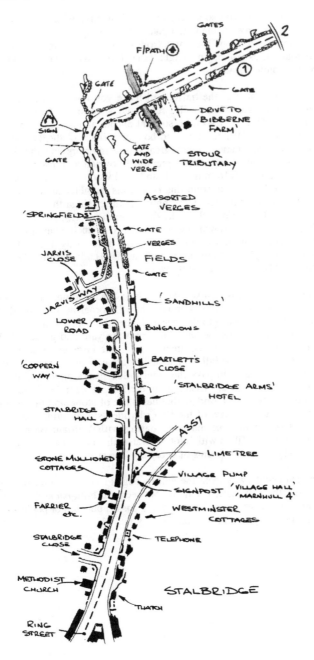

DAY 6 - STAGE 2

BIBBERNE FARM TO BAGBER

Uphill slightly now, you soon reach a LH farm drive which leads down to Bungays Farm and, on the brow of the hill, a gate with a Footpath arrow leads into a RH field with a mixed wood about 100 yards from the road. There are fine, pastoral views over on your left as you begin a slight descent towards the cross-roads which you can see about 1/4 mile ahead.

As I mentioned, most of the traffic will leave you now to turn right to Sturminster Newton or left to cross Kings Mill Bridge into Marnhull. Cross "Kings Mill Road" and you will find the next section, straight ahead, almost deserted. The iron fence which borders the RH field is the old boundary fence of the Thornhill House Estate. Sir James Thornhill painted many great house interiors and the dome of St Paul's Cathedral and bought this estate - previously owned and lost by his ancestors - in 1725 with the proceeds from his skill and hard work. He designed and built a fine Palladian-style house and, from this house, his daughter married one of Thornhill's pupils - none other than that great English painter, Hogarth - realistic painter of the street life of old London such as the degradation of "Gin Alley". It's strange to consider the artistic skills which were developed in such a small concentrated area of Dorset including Thornhill and Hogarth 1/4 mile away from this spot, William Barnes born at Bagber 3/4 mile away and Thomas Hardy writing 'Return of the Native' at Sturminster Newton 2.1/2 miles away.

However, follow the now sparsely-verged lane down and up, past gates on either side, to a gate and entrance to Marsh Farm on the LH corner of a RH bend in the lane near the brow of the hill. Keep to the lane and, after the concrete drive to Ryalls Farm on the top of the hill, follow the lane down past the yard and garden of the stone house on your left, past two large ash trees, a gate, one large oak tree and a wide, grassy verge at the bottom of the hill. The hedges are now on banks in the dip and the lane is a little narrower as you pass the steel-railed banks approaching Bagber Bridge. The stile on your right is Private, as is the fishing - for "Stalbridge A.C. Members Only" - on the left. The bridge abutments are of stone and the centre rails are cast iron whilst the restful view of the River Lydden slowly gliding Northwards towards the Stour is one which we must be sharing with William Barnes himself. The downriver section is filled with 'clotes' (water lilies) and these are often mentioned in Barnes' wryly observant poems of everyday Dorset life.

Now, drag yourself away from the willow-edged river and, after the gate into the LH field, follow the very narrow lane up between the high-banked, hedged fields to the LH turning to Bagber House Farm - having passed bunches of poplars and the sign for "Bagber", probably overgrown, on the way up.

118

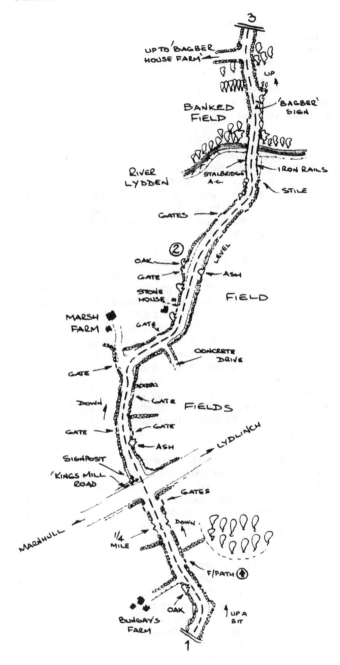

DAY 6 - STAGE 3

BAGBER TO MILL LANE

There isn't much left of the hamlet of Bagber where William Barnes was born, the son of a yeoman farmer. The registration of his birth in March 1801 only gives his place of birth as Number 7, Bagber but many of the smaller farm cottages have long since disappeared. His daughter, Lucy Baxter, recalled that William was born on a farm called Rushay and there still exists a farmhouse of this name, just of the drove to Bagber Common, but it isn't the original building. But young William would definitely have known the Manor House which stands at the beginning of the ancient track to Sturminster Mill, just on the next bend of this country lane.

There are gates into all of the fields which border the junction after "Manor Farmhouse" on the right. Where the lane begins a RH bend, turn left onto the track which emerges, between a gated turning to some low barns and a grass island with its own post box, to join your lane. The tarmac track is signed "No Through Road" but this only means for vehicles and a later signpost confirms that this is a "Halter Path to Sturminster Newton". As you join the track, the first gates lead into the present farmyard whilst the neat grass verge with the iron chains and the high wall are all protecting the fine old stone "Manor House".

As you progress up this track, the tarmac runs out and, after right and left gates, the banked hedges get higher above the bottom of the track. On the way, the hedge is mostly of hawthorn with oak and ash trees spreading over your head but, after gates to left and right at the top of the rise, you begin to descend between beech hedges. At the bottom of the track, there is a gate on the right and another track goes left to a gated field. Keep straight on, now slightly upwards, with a low field on the left and a high field on the right, both behind beech hedges interspersed with ash, oak and sycamores. Suddenly, the track turns towards a gate into the LH field, with another gate on the right. Keep straight on, though, down into a wide, deep, grassy hollow-way with pebbles underfoot like the bed of a stream. The path may be narrower but, without the undergrowth and intruding trees, the lane would be just as wide as before. This must have been a busy route between Sturminster Mill, Bagber, Stalbridge and beyond. It is deeply worn by carts delivering corn to the Mill and collecting the finished flour.

To prevent illegal wheeled traffic about 100 yards into this track, there are now twin posts of solid iron rail track guarding the central portion of the path and the track is quite narrow between these sets of posts but, emerging from the other end, between hawthorns and sycamores, the track widens again. Go past two gates into opposite fields and over an iron-railed, concrete bridge which spans the River Divelish on its Northward route to join the Stour. Willows and beeches line its banks in either direction.´

After the LH field gate, follow the narrowing grass track up past another pair of gates, with a high field on the left and a banked hedge on the right. A large oak overhangs the path from your left and, after another oak in the RH bank, there is a plethora of gates either side of the route. The two largest gates on the right lead into an area of barns, followed by a 'ski-jump'. Keep on, past a house with a cattle grid guarding its entrance, to a section of wooden fences with another cattle grid, a couple of gates and a Footpath-signed stile on the right. A gated, concrete drive an the left leads, between the garden fence and a wooden fenced field, to more barns.

THE BLACKMORE VALE PATH

DAY 6 - STAGE 3

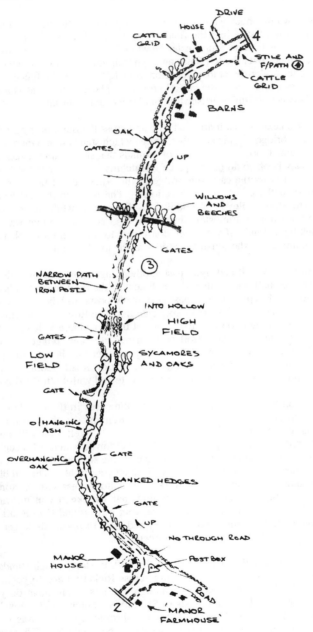

DAY 6 - STAGE 4

MILL LANE TO STURMINSTER NEWTON

Keep on down the much wider track, past a large oak on the right, to the first gate and Footpath-arrowed stile into the field on your left where a Footpath post points to "Colber Bridge 1/4 and Sturminster Newton 1/2". Go over the stile into the field with a few pines over the RH fence and, ignoring the clearer track which heads to one of the arches under the embankment on your left, follow the fence, hedge and ditch round to a gate and stile in the far RH corner. The embankment is a remnant of the railway between Sturminster Newton, Stalbridge and Wincanton.

Go over this next Footpath-arrowed stile and cross the field, bearing left, towards the painted iron bridge. This is Colber Bridge which stands where there was "anciently a manor or hamlet, now only a parcel of grounds that still retain the name. *Colesberie* in Domesday book could be this place": Hutchins. Go over the stile or through the half-gate and cross the cast-iron bridge to the other side of the River Stour where a selection of paths go off in all directions. The paths to the left head upstream to follow "The Stour Valley Path" (Book 1 in this series) whilst all of the paths to the right lead down to Sturminster Newton Mill. You can go all that way, following the river bank for 1/2 mile, if you really don't want to see Sturminster Newton at all, but I would recommend a short visit to "Stur" - as the locals call it.

Past all turnings to left and right, past another finger-post and over the arrowed stile next to another half-gate, follow the path next to the right fence and hedge, uphill on a RH bearing. Keep on uphill, past two arrow posts, to where the concrete wall of the gardens at the top joins the kissing gate into The Row. Now, tidy yourself up a bit as you're coming into the market town of the Blackmore Vale (The Market is on a Monday) and enjoy an easy stroll past various pleasant cottages to where the road turns left towards Sturminster Hall. Keep straight on, though, and you'll arrive at the end of The Row into Market Place with Station Road leading to the Market, the Car Park and the B3091 to Shaftesbury opposite and with Bath Road going left.

Turn right, on the pavement, towards the parking area in the middle of Market Place with the "Swan Inn" over on your left. Remember what I said about buying something at every village shop which you find. Well, you will sometimes come across a 'village' type shop in these old market towns which still keep the traditions of service to the community very much alive. One such exists just along here where the main street narrows before Gough's Close on your right. The old black and white shop of Candy's Newsagents and Stores is the epitomy of a village store and I would recommend a visit. They sell everything that will keep you informed of events world-wide, all that you'll ever need to find your way around Dorset, all the chocolate you'll need to sustain you on your journey and loads of postcards to send to the folks back home - and all under one, very low ceiling.

Past Candy's, follow the main road past the "White Hart" which stands opposite the remnants of Sturminster town cross, and across Ricketts Lane to begin your descent towards the Mill. Before you leave, though, the raised pavement on your left leads to Church Lane which, in turn, leads to St Mary's Church. This lovely church was originally built by John Selwood, abbot of Glastonbury, but it was rebuilt in 1827, except for the original tower, at the expense of the curate Rev. Thomas Lane-Fox of Hinton St Mary, in the 14th Century style. Thomas Dashwood, solicitor and William Barnes' first employer - as a clerk - is buried here.

THE BLACKMORE VALE PATH

DAY 6 - STAGE 4

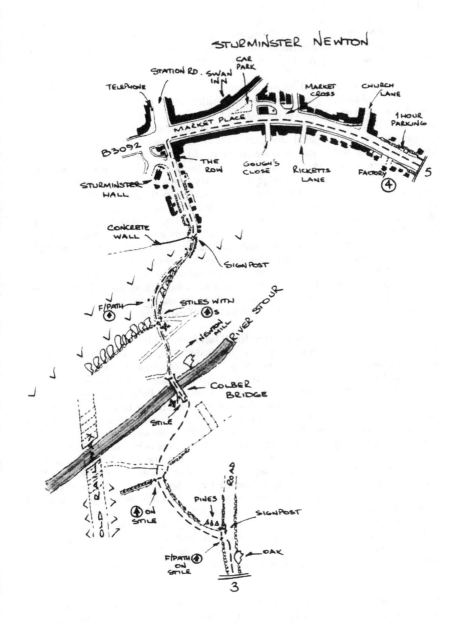

DAY 6 - STAGE 5

STURMINSTER NEWTON TO BROAD OAK PATH

By now, you will be following the road out of Stur, down past a couple of 1-hour parking spaces and a fine stone house over on the left (no pavement) and past a factory and "The Cottage" on your right.   Before you leave altogether, there is no mention of Sturminster in the Domesday Book although its sister settlement of Newton, on the other side of the six-arched medieval bridge, is listed as "the Church of St Mary, Glastonbury holds *Newentone*". - More later.

For now, cross Durrant and follow the pavement with a low field on your right and with a gate and kissing gate onto a riverside path in the deep hedge on your left.   A row of poplars marks the end of the RH field, just opposite a traffic light, and, as you begin to walk along the land arches which were added to the bridge in 1825, you will see Sturminster Newton Mill along the river bank to your right.   Go through the kissing gate next to the gate into the meadow and follow the signed path along the LH fence, over two drainage channels, towards the Mill.   At the end of the fence, where the path from "Colber Bridge 1/2" comes down the field on your right, go through the kissing gate by the Footpath post and follow the path over a concrete and steel-railed footbridge and past steps up to a private gate.   After the weir and the sluice gates between the high and low levels of the Stour, follow the path round the back of the Mill, past a stile and steps up to the car park.   Most of the Mill is late 17th Century and, on the main door jamb, you can see flood levels of 1756 and 1979. Leave the Mill by continuing up the tarmac lane with the car park up on your right and the Stour down on your left.   There are two benches on the top bank as you leave the Mill lane and turn left to join the A357 so a rest overlooking the willow trees and river may be permitted.   After that, keep on down the main road and, before you reach the medieval bridge, cross over the A357 to the RH pavement.

At the Footpath signpost and the sign for "Sturminster Mill 150 yards", turn up the narrow lane past the red-brick, Primitive Methodist Chapel of 1870 and the similar house beyond it.   Then, where the old path is marked with an old sign "Danger. Footpath Closed" turn left and climb the steps up and round to the Footpath-arrowed stile at the top.   Go over the stile into the high and quiet field, away from the noise of the traffic on the main road below. Keep near to the LH wire fence and hedge, with two houses and a small paddock over on your right.   Go over the stile in the facing wire fence, about 30 yards from the gate in the LH corner and cross the next small field to another farm gate near the LH corner.   A signpost points on to "Hole House Lane 1/4" and right to "Glue Hill 1/4".   Cross the dip into the LH valley and keep straight on, next to the fence with oaks, beeches and sycamores on a bank.   Follow the fence and trees slightly upwards around the field edge and before the next fence, a Footpath-arrowed stile leads onto a narrow path with beech hedges either side whilst there is the slate roof of a house in the steep drop on your left.   In a few yards, at the end of the path, the gateway into this house's drive shows that this is "Hole House" and a larger track passes from left to right at the end of your exit (which is signed "Town Bridge 1/2").   Therefore, this is Hole House Lane.   Turn sharp left, not on the larger track, and go down the path next to Hole House's hedge, signed "Broad Oak 1/2".

Keep on down the shale path into a valley and cross the small bridge across a stream which runs from left to right into the high-banked darkness.   Follow the steps cut into the steep bank and enter a long, upward-sloping field through a kissing gate.

124

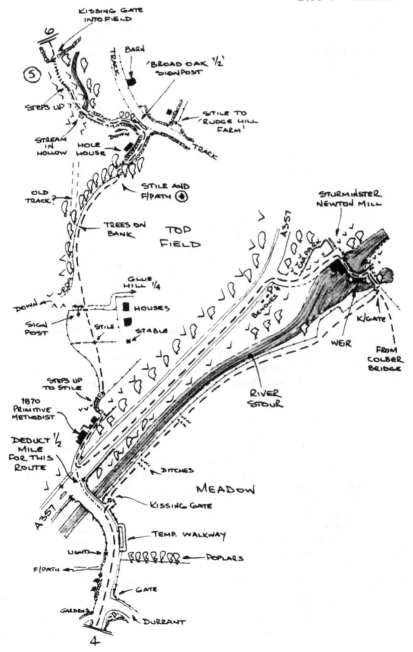

KISSING GATE
INTO FIELD

BARN

TRACK

'BROAD OAK ½'
SIGNPOST

⑤

STEPS UP

STILE TO
'RUDGE HILL
FARM'

STREAM
IN
HOLLOW

HOLE
HOUSE

DOWN

TRACK

OLD
TRACK?

STILE AND
F/PATH ⊕

TREES ON
BANK

TOP
FIELD

STURMINSTER
NEWTON MILL

A357

CAR PARK

CLUB
HILL ¼

HOUSES

DOWN

SIGN
POST

STILE

STABLE

BENDS?

K/GATE

WEIR

FROM
COLBER
BRIDGE

STEPS UP
TO STILE

RIVER
STOUR

1870
PRIMITIVE
METHODIST

DEDUCT ½
MILE
FOR THIS
ROUTE

DITCHES

MEADOW

KISSING GATE

A357

TEMP. WALKWAY

LIGHTS

POPLARS

F/PATH

GATE

GARDENS

DURRANT

4

DAY 6 - STAGE 6

BROAD OAK PATH TO OKEFORD HOLLOW-WAY

I hate having to do this but there wasn't enough space on the last Stage to tell you about the Newton part of Sturminster Newton when you arrived in the high field after the Primitive Methodist Chapel.   But, as you wander up the faint path to Broad Oak at the top of this field, let me go back a bit to when there was more to Newton than there is now.   At the dissolution of the monasteries in 1538, a certificate of survey stated of the old manor of Newton - "the scite of the said house standeth upon a high hill, just by a great running river in the vally.   It is of th'aunyent buylding, portly and strong, able and mete for a knight to lye in".   Of the castle, Camden described it as - "a mole of earth which cost no small pains in throwing up - but nothing remains of the castle but the name".   But he did notice a 'deep and wide ditch which is 350 feet long, varying from 30-40 feet deep, running nearly East and West.   Could this have been the wide cutting which crossed our path into the last field?   The castle probably existed in Saxon times but fell into ruin in 12th/13th Century whilst a few remains of Early-English character existed until the mid-1800s.

That's better.   I didn't want to leave it out altogether and this is quite a long, uphill field.   Now, near the top, bear right after the big oak in the LH hedge and go through the Footpath-arrowed gate into a grassy area between two gardens.   This leads out into the village of Broad Oak, somewhat expanded during recent years by new housing.   A direction post points back to "Hole House Lane 1/2".   On the road through the village, turn left and then instantly right, uphill with new houses on the left.   Go past a cottage, a bungalow and a double-gated, rough downhill drive on the left and a hedge with oaks and ashes on the right.   After gates to Sheerbrow Farm on the right and to some barns on the left, you reach the top of the hill and some more gates to cattle sheds on your right.   There is a signpost to "Broad Oak 1/4" leading into the RH yard - but watch out for goats if you ever go that way.   There is another signpost near a bench at the gate on your left but keep straight on, down the pleasant, shady tree-lined lane through Piddles Wood - mostly oak but with some ash and small beech trees as well.

The lane is quite steep now as you come out of the woods to find a stile in the first RH hedge with a direction arrow to "Dirty Gate 1/4".   Keep on down, between hedged fields and ditches and with a fine view towards Hambledon Hill beyond the hedge oaks on your left.   A gate leads to a Dutch barn on your right and, just after a RH lay-by, you arrive at a T-junction.   The RH turn leads to Banbury Hill-fort, an ancient British circular camp, about 300 yards in diameter but now almost obliterated, whilst the LH lane goes to Angiers Farm, site of a fairly large village until June 1729 when a great fire "consumed, by 12 a.m., 67 dwelling houses, 10 barns and stables and outhouses and the market house": Hutchins.   Cross over, straight onto a rough grass track with gates into fields on either side - the RH entrance leading to a vast layout of poly-tunnels.   As the rough track turns to a gate in the LH hawthorn hedge, with a few oak trees on your right, go into a narrow, tree-lined hollow-way with river-bed pebbles underfoot.   After a plank bridge to keep you out of the mud in the dip, followed by a half-gate on your right, the path begins to climb between high fields with many oaks, moss and various ferns in the steep banks.   After a ditch runs into our path from a high RH field,, you emerge onto a lighter, wider track which emanates from the farm gate round the RH corner.   Keep straight on, past another RH gate and between oak and ash trees.

DAY 6 - STAGE 7

OKEFORD HOLLOW-WAY TO OKEFORD FITZPAINE

This end of the ancient hollow-way has expanded over the years into a farm track but it is still several feet below the level of the adjoining fields. Going slightly downhill, as the track bears slightly right, you pass a concrete track to Darknoll Farm. Follow the main track down, past opposite gates and into a willow-edged dip where a small stream sometimes floods across the path on its way to the Stour. The track is now becoming an old tarmac lane as you ascend between vertical banks with oaks and ashes on top. The pair of wooden gates into a lovely garden on your right signal your entry into Okeford Fitzpaine whilst a selection of barns and stables on your left are opposed by the beautiful stone, red-brick and thatched house of Etheridge Farm on your right. Carry on down the lane, past stiles on either side before a bridge over a second Stour-bound stream. Past houses on both sides, you soon emerge, past "Darknoll Lane" and "Halter Path to Sturminster Newton" signs.

Cross over the road to the pavement on the other side and turn left. Follow the lane into the village, past Bowey on your right and past the deserted Wesleyan Methodist Chapel of 1830. Keep straight on past houses and cottages of all ages and styles, but mostly 18th Century, noting especially Easter Cottage and Duck Cottage on the left before Castle Avenue and the pillared Stresa House and Hillview Farmhouse on your right. At the T-junction, with the "Royal Oak" on the LH corner, turn right along the high garden wall, opposite the village school and the green telephone box. The Dorset CC signpost (807110) points around the sweeping left bend to "Blandford Forum". Follow the pavement round, via the Post Office for a can of drink or a bar of chocolate which you can devour on the bench opposite. I know you've spent nearly all of your money at the village stores which we've passed already but it's all in a good cause and this *is* the last one before Blandford and you *are* going to sit down and read about Okeford Fitzpaine, aren't you..

In the Domesday Book as *Adford*, held by the church of St Mary, Glastonbury, Okeford Fitzpaine has previously been Ockford Alured (from the usual christian name, Alured, of the ruling DeLincolnias) and Ockford Nichole (from the surname of a later, French, ruling lord) but it has been Okeford Fitzpaine since Edward I who granted Robert Fitzpaine a charter to hold markets and fairs. There is a fine rectory and 14th Century church - but we'll see those in a minute.

Now, refreshed again, keep to the raised pavement, with thatched cottages on both sides of the road, to the next junction with the vast mid-18th Century Georgian rectory and an equally vast cedar in its garden behind the fine brick wall. Here, the road bends left to Shillingstone and Blandford Forum with Back Lane turning around the cemetery wall whilst the lane on your right leads "To Greenhayes". You want none of these. Instead, go quietly through a kissing gate by the side of the lych gate into St Andrew's Church.

There has been a church on this site since at least the early 12th Century when, in the Register of Simon of Gaunt, Bishop of Salisbury, the rector was ordered to have the church ready for consecration during the week following St James Day - July 25th 1302. The 14th Century replacement was extended in Tudor times and much of the materials used in the 1866 rebuild (by Hardy's first employer, architect John Hicks) date from these periods. The triangular Victorian font, with an angel on each corner, is particularly beautiful and looks as if it could have been carved yesterday.

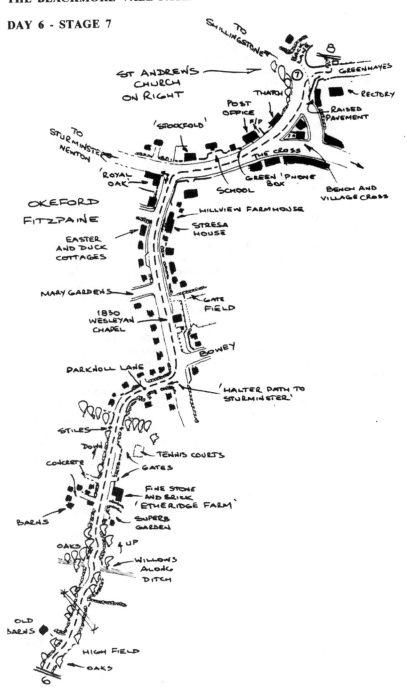

TO SHILLINGSTONE

8

GREENHAYES

ST ANDREWS
CHURCH
ON RIGHT

THATCH

RECTORY

POST
OFFICE

P/P

RAISED
PAVEMENT

'STOCKFOLD'

TO
STURMINSTER
NEWTON

THE CROSS

'ROYAL
OAK'

GREEN 'PHONE
BOX

BENCH AND
VILLAGE CROSS

SCHOOL

OKEFORD
FITZPAINE

HILLVIEW FARMHOUSE

STRESA
HOUSE

EASTER
AND DUCK
COTTAGES

MARY GARDENS

GATE
FIELD

1830
WESLEYAN
CHAPEL

BOWEY

DARKNOLL LANE

'HALTER PATH TO
STURMINSTER'

STILES

DOWN

TENNIS COURTS

CONCRETE
GATES

FINE STONE
AND BRICK
'ETHERIDGE FARM'

BARNS

SUPERB
GARDEN

OAKS

UP

WILLOWS
ALONG
DITCH

OLD
BARNS

HIGH FIELD

OAKS

6

129

DAY 6 - STAGE 8

OKEFORD FITZPAINE TO OKEFORD HILL

Leave St Andrew's Churchyard through the kissing gate onto Back Lane and turn right. A farm track, signposted for "Shillingstone 1/4", descends to your left but follow the lane up past a few cottages on your left to the last, unique cottage. If, as they say, "necessity is the mother of invention", she must surely be the favourite aunt of DIY vehicle maintenance. Here lives a familiar figure to all who live in Okeford Fitzpaine - Geoffrey Ricketts who, with his colleague Maurice Matthews, is locally famous for driving around on a three-wheeled, general purpose truck which he uses to collect firewood and whatever items he might need to maintain or repair all manner of machinery. The pair of them even starred in ITV's 'Country Ways' a few years ago with a fascinating demonstration of ferreting techniques. However, passing by the remnants of stripped vehicles and 'useful items', turn left when you get to the top of the lane.

You are now on a gravely track with a banked hedge on your right and scattered trees in the LH hedge. Follow the track uphill and, at the first gap, have a look at the scarp and Shillingstone chalk quarry. You remember the explanation for the swallow holes (the acidic water dissolving the underlying chalk). Well, the acidic run-off from the rough grass and ancient heath made the arable land at the foot of the escarpment very acidic as well. The chalk was taken to be spread onto the fields to reduce this acidity - but it has since been quarried extensively for lime to make the lime-mortar needed to lay the relatively soft local building stone.

Continue up the hill and go through the gate across the track onto the grazing pastures of Okeford Hill. Keep ascending, past the old quarry face on your right, and follow the higher and clearer of two narrow paths past the far corner of the grass-covered water tank enclosure. There is no way you could get this far without stopping innumerable times to look back over the vast panorama opening out behind you as you climb. This is the point where you begin to realise that the walk is nearly over and that you have wandered freely over much of the Vale spread out below. On a clear day, you can see Wales from here but, more usually, Sherborne, King Alfred's Tower at Stourhead, Shaftesbury, Fontmell Down and the edge of Cranborne Chase all stand out in the distance whilst Hambledon Hill, Child Okeford and Okeford Fitzpaine are in the nearer view.

When you reach the top corner of this vast, fenced field, a gate leads out onto the Winterborne Stickland to Okeford Fitzpaine road and, if you go through and up to the gate on the other side of the road, you will have clear views along the escarpment to the West. And what is that tree-clad point far beyond the scarp on which you are standing? It's High Stoy, from where we had our first real sight of the Vale on the lane up from Minterne Magna on Day 4 - Stage 1. However, I'll leave you to make your own discoveries with the aid of OS Map No. 194 - but it's still five miles to Blandford.

Back to the top field, go through the gate into the next field and follow the clear path across and up to the next 3/4 size gate (no arrows). Through this gate, follow the same line on an upward bearing, with the beacon, which was part of the 1988 national celebrations of the 1588 Defeat of the Spanish Armada, up on the right.

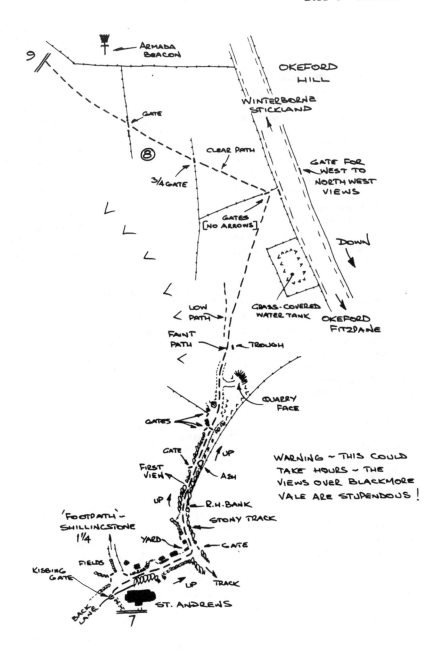

9

ARMADA BEACON

OKEFORD HILL

WINTERBORNE STICKLAND

GATE

⑧

CLEAR PATH

GATE FOR WEST TO NORTH WEST VIEWS

¾ GATE

GATES [NO ARROWS]

DOWN

LOW PATH

GRASS-COVERED WATER TANK

OKEFORD FITZPANE

FAINT PATH

TROUGH

QUARRY FACE

GATES

CATE

UP

FIRST VIEW

ASH

WARNING ~ THIS COULD TAKE HOURS ~ THE VIEWS OVER BLACKMORE VALE ARE STUPENDOUS !

UP

R.H. BANK

'FOOTPATH'- SHILLINGSTONE 1¼

STONY TRACK

YARD

GATE

FIELDS

KISSING GATE

UP

TRACK

BACK LANE

ST. ANDREWS

7

DAY 6 - STAGE 9

OKEFORD HILL TO BONSLEY COMMON

You have just come up about 500 feet from Okeford Fitzpaine and, once you enter the woods facing you now, you have a 600 feet descent to Blandford Forum. As this is over a distance of some 4.1/2 miles, the descent is long, consistent and gradual.

Keep to your current direction, on the level and gradually closing with the top fence, and you will arrive in the far right corner where a gate leads out of your field. Here, with a gravel track running away to your right, go past the wooden posts and the barrier, straight on, onto a peaty path which runs along a wide, down-sloping, grassy ride through the wood of mixed pines and beeches with ferns and foxgloves all around. At the first crossing of tracks, as the main ride goes straight on, take the wide, grassy turn up to the right and you will emerge onto a triangle of rough, open ground with gorse, long grass and bracken. A post on the immediate RH corner carries Wessex Ridgeway and DCC arrows for the track which you are about to cross.

Beyond this crossing, almost in a straight line with your arrival, a grass path goes off with the the edge of the wood on its right (this is the one you want) whilst a wider, short section crosses the triangle and goes towards a vast field. "This is probably the last remnant of the original common as it may have looked before afforestation: DCC Guide.

Take the more-or-less straight-on path which I have already mentioned with bracken on the left and the woods on the right and follow this narrow path which runs within a wider grass track all the way down to a half gate in the hedge directly in front of you. All this time, the vast field is beyond the grass and bracken strip on your left. Go through the unmarked metal gate and turn left in the field on the other side. Follow the hedge on the LH edge of this field down to a full-size, unmarked gate next to a holly tree in a wire fence between this and the next field. After the gate, follow the LH hedge of hawthorn and beech, on a wide cut track, all the way to the bottom end of the field where another track emerges through the hedge from your left.

Keep straight on down to the next gate which leads into the edge of the mainly beech woods. The open canopy of the beech wood on your left encourages a healthy undergrowth which includes primroses, bluebells and wild garlic whilst the trees between you and the field on your right are mainly hazel, coppiced for hurdle-making and for spars, slats and liggers (fixing strips for thatching).

Keep on down this clear, peaty path, now with some ash trees, pines and bracken, followed by oaks, sycamores, beech and more ash (in fact, everything ancient woods should have), until a narrow path comes out from the woods on your left. At this point, I was aware of some head-banging going on up the trees overhead and, having seen that woodpecker near Rue Farm on Day 5, I searched above me in the hope of seeing another one. However, the bird I saw was smaller and was putting his whole body into the attack on the tree - not just his head and shoulders like the woodpecker. He was slate-grey on top and creamy yellow underneath - a fine, very busy, nuthatch.

Keep on down the track, leaving Bonsley Common woods behind you and entering a narrow path between a wire-fenced field on your left and a narrow, tree-filled area with a field beyond it on your RH side. From the corner of the LH field - on a clear day - you can see the Isle of Wight beyond Shepherds Corner Farm in the dip.

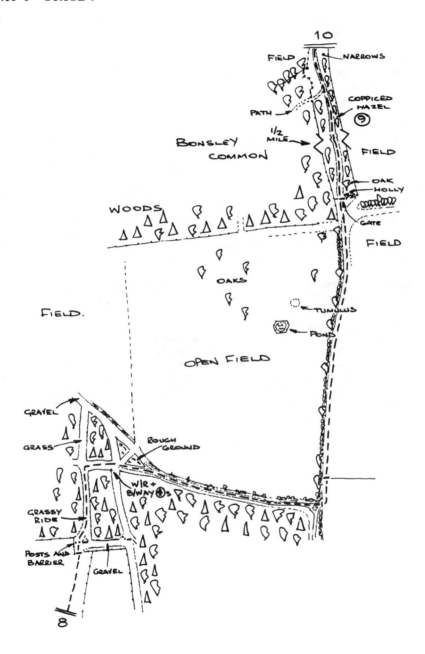

BONSLEY COMMON TO FIELD GROVE

In just a little over 1/4 mile of easy, slightly downhill walking on a narrowing, sometimes lumpy path, you reach a cross-tracks where the major track goes right, between hawthorn and beech hedges.   Where the 'Jubilee Trail' arrow directs, go through the gate across the LH turning and cross over to go straight on, through another gate with a 'J/Tr' arrow to the left of a large sycamore and an ash tree.   This leads to a large, level field with a cut track running along its RH hedge, first passing a large crab-apple tree.   I know they make a lot of cider around here, but this tree seems to be a long way from the production areas.   I wonder how it got here.   Anyway, follow the fenced, rabbit hole-filled hedge to the far end where, under an electricity pole, another 'J/Tr'-arrowed gate leads into a smaller, left-rising field.   Again, follow the RH hedge to the other end where, past a single oak and a holly tree, a 'J/Tr'-signed half- gate leads into the deep oak and beech Field Grove wood.

Here again, the trees on the right are coppiced hazel between the path and a field whilst the peat and gravel path glides down, past a couple of LH grass tracks, to a LH wide forest ride between ranks of pine trees.   Contrast again, if you will, the dark and dead floor beneath these leafless pine trees with the healthy floor beneath the hardwoods on your right.   The pines are planted in a series of parallel lines with access tracks in between - very boring.

After a 'J/Tr'-signed grassy ride turns up to your right and an overgrown grass track goes left, our track becomes wide gravel with oaks on the left and almost completely oaks, after some beech and pines, on the right.   So, enjoy the airy, gentle stroll through the fresh woodland air whilst you can.   It does wonders for the health - and the soul - and the Blackmore Vale Path is rapidly drawing to its close.   We could do with a few uphill paths to slow us down.   But there aren't any.   The next right turning grass track has three 'J/Tr' arrows - two on a LH pine (safe at least until it's harvested) and one on a RH post.   Keep straight on, between foxgloves, bracken, pines and beeches and oaks, through this 3/4 mile long wood and, after a wooden barrier crosses your path, a solitary house stands atop a rise on your left behind a wood-fenced paddock.

Keep going, passing a gated track which turns back on your right.

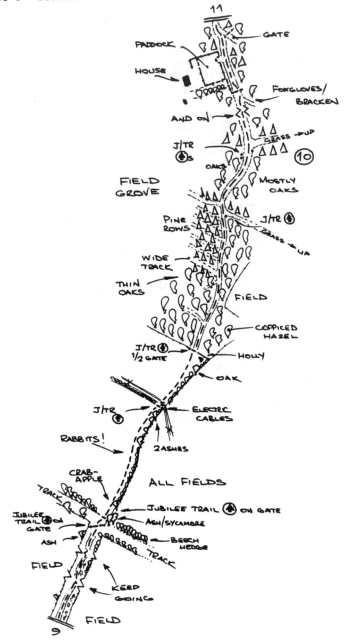

DAY 6 - STAGE 11

FIELD GROVE TO SHOTHOLE

In a few yards, you leave Field Grove as the track reaches a farm track coming from the left and heading, through a gate down on the right, onto a "Private - Farm Track Only". As you weave past the barrier across your track, a Bridleway arrow and another 'J/Tr' arrow point up the track which doubles back into the field to your right. Don't take any of the directions which I have already mentioned. Cross over to the flinty, left track which goes uphill into another wood, past the edge of a gate and between banks. There. No sooner do I ask for something to slow the approaching end, than a hill presents itself - albeit a very short one. There is a lovely, dark hollow on your right - filled with deep, dense harts-tongue ferns. The conditions must be perfect for them in there. In fact, they have spread into the banks alongside our path, together with the more usual ferns.

After a grassy track goes left, you reach the top of this climb and join the path which is enclosed between the fenced LH wood and the wire-fenced RH vast field. At one time, the Bridleway went straight across this field but we are now entrained all around the edge of it - adding nearly 1/4 mile to the crossing. Over on your left, you can see the tall mast which you saw en route to Winterborne Stickland, not long after you left Blandford on Day 1. Just follow the long, level path, passing a wide, grassy ride through the LH strip of woods near the end of the path. At the very end, go through the wooden half-gate posts onto a sharp bend in the country road. Carefully now, there are cars about between Winterborne Stickland and Blandford or Durweston.

Turn left and keep close to, or on, the LH bank - there isn't much protection afforded by the narrow verge against Broadley Wood over on the right. In about 1/4 mile, a notice around the LH corner shows that this is all Broadley Wood, part of the Wareham Forest - and Wareham is miles from here. However, with the corner verge giving more security, you can look around and see Blandford Forum down in the valley and Bryanston School over on your left. The road sign points to "Durweston" up to the left, "Bryanston and Blandford Forum" straight on and "Winterborne Stickland" behind you. Keep straight on, along the road, now over on the RH side to face any oncoming vehicles. After a single house on the right, a gravel track turns right to past the garden hedge and a tarmac track goes down to some brick and flint cottages on the left. If you look down the valley side, you will see the strip lynchets of an ancient field system.

Keep following the strip of mixed beech, ash, pine and sycamore trees on the RH side of the road, very gently uphill and past a turning with a barrier onto a RH track. Shortly after that, a grass track leads to a gate into the field beyond the trees and the road bears slightly left.

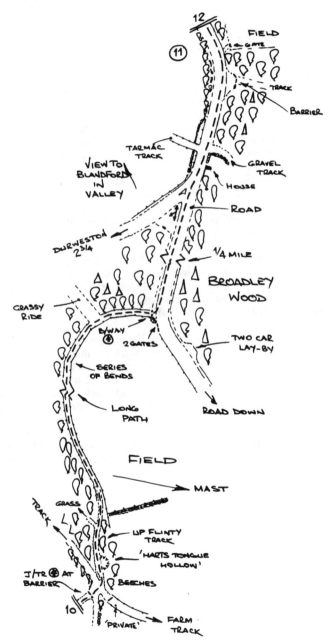

DAY 6 - STAGES 12 AND 13

SHOTHOLE TO BEECH CLUMP TO BLANDFORD FORUM

Not long now.   Another 1/4 mile and we'll be rejoining the departure route at Quarleston Down.   Carry on along the road to the first RH turning facing a gate over on your left and with a brick cottage on the far corner.   Turn right, past the corner gate, and follow the tarmac lane between the low flint and brick wall before the cottages on the left and the hedgerow on the right.   A driveway leads to the red brick house and outbuildings of Quarleston Kennels on your left, as does a wider, wood-fenced drive a few yards further down the lane.

This used to be another of the Winterborne villages - Winterborne Quarleston, which was once a separate vill (a small group of houses) and manor.   Already a farm in Hutchin's time, it receives its name from the Quarrels, once lords of the manor.   In the 13th year of Edward III's reign (1340), this was the seat of William de Quarrel. Originally, Quarrelston House was an old, low building, forming a quadrangle but, in the early 19th Century, a great part of it was demolished.

Past all of the present buildings, go through a gate across the lane into the massed gates of the four-way junction of Day 1 - Stage 2.

As you stand in this area of gates, bear a little left on the downhill track to go past the barns at the side of the track and you will recognize where you are.   However, I'm not going to ask you to find your way back by following the Stage Maps which we used on the way here.   Oh, No.   I'm much too kind.   The route is repeated on Stage 6 - Maps 12 and 13 - the right way up.   So, off you go!

Now, what more is there to say as you follow the maps back to Blandford.   I could only repeat what I've told you already in these first/last 2 miles.   However, when you reach Blandford, you will know that you've circumnavigated Blackmore Vale and seen some of the loveliest villages and hidden spots of Dorset which will remain largely unknown to those less enamoured of the "feet on" approach.   (I'm sure that, with the rash of computer language with which we are currently being assailed, that is what walking will be called in the near future).

It's still all downhill from here, so enjoy your triumphant arrival into Blandford Forum and, after 71 miles, you'll at least know why you ache.   See you shortly on another "Path".

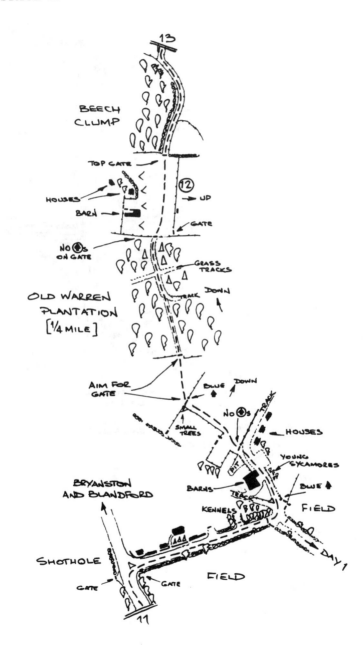

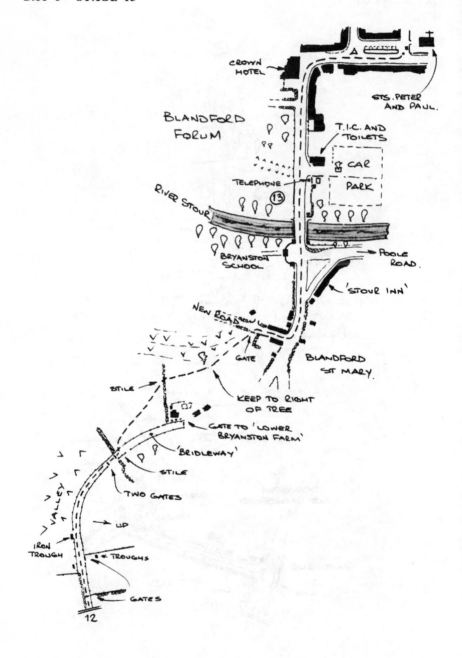

THE BLACKMORE VALE PATH

IN CONCLUSION

This third long-distance Path was so long in the planning that, when I actually set out from Blandford on the first day of exploration, I could not imagine what a wonderful, pleasure-packed walk lay ahead of me.   Having lived in Dorset for 30 years, I had visited some of the villages and all of the towns on the route but only by car.   As I said when introducing "The Cranborne Chase Path", - "...glimpses through car or coach windows can offer no more than a fleeting enjoyment of anywhere" and this is especially true of this walk around and across Blackmore Vale.   I have found places of such wonder that I have been loathe to leave them but, not long afterwards, I have wandered into something completely different but no less enchanting.   For example, I have been a lover of the Lake District fells (Cumbria) for many years but, in the foothills, one of my favourite strolls is through the Whinlatter Pass Forest.   On the first Day of this walk, when I entered Charity Wood, just before Milton Abbas, the twisting tracks, the footpath which plunged into the woods, the quarry-like banks of fern on the edges of the tracks and the wonderful smell of pine in the air all reminded me of Whinlatter Pass.   Absolute heaven.

The downland paths, on grazing land and through cornfields, have all offered fine views and promises of the lush river valleys and the beautiful, stone-built villages which are scattered about Blackmore Vale.   The fresh air of the downs is quite bracing whilst the warmer air of the Vale is almost soporific.   It isn't just the views or the charm of the villages - it's the smells.   As I've already said, the woods are filled with the smell of pine but, there are other wonderful smells along the way.   Depending on when you go, there is honeysuckle, cut meadow grass and cereal crops in the summer and there is the lush damp smell of the hedges and the curry-like smell of the drying hogweed in the verges in the autumn.   In the spring, there are bluebells and ramson (wild garlic), followed by carpets of foxgloves.

It would take another book to list all of the delights which particularly appealed to me but my real purpose was to show you how to find your way, on foot, around the Vale and where to find representative samples of what Blackmore Vale has to offer the observant explorer.   Briefly, though, I suppose the highlights for me have to include the corner towns themselves (and in these we must include Sherborne which was to have been one of the corners, originally) and the intermediate towns of Stalbridge and Sturminster Newton.   The villages - Milton Abbas, Tolpuddle, The Bockhamptons, Cerne Abbas, Minterne Magna, Leigh, Yetminster, Barwick, Okeford Fitzpaine - all had individual appeal but I found Yetminster to be the most exciting, notwithstanding the whippet with a bootlace fetish at Petties Farm.   I loved the great houses such as Milton Abbas, Minterne Magna and Sherborne Castle - or their remains - as at Clifton Maubank, Barwick House and Sherborne Old Castle.

The arrivals through forests into Milton Abbas and to Hardy's Cottage were both something special and I loved coming across unexpected links with the great and good of the past.   Robert Boyle's School in Yetminster came as a complete surprise to me - as did his Irish ancestry and his links with Stalbridge Mansion.   To me, he had always been a name synonymous with physics and nothing else.   And it was a great pleasure to find the Yetminster farm where Benjamin Jesty lived and worked and where he formed his idea for inoculation against smallpox.

I enjoyed the follies of Barwick, near Yeovil (especially Jack the Treacle Eater) and the arrival into Yeovil down Nine Springs. After Yeovil, I was quite taken with the deep, sandstone Bradford Hollow gorge which runs up to the Bradford Abbas top road, followed by the high country lane and the pastoral idyll between Yeovil and the lovely, mellow and learned town of Sherborne.

Having found "Roman Building" on my map along that top lane, I really enjoyed delving into the old Reports of the Dorset Antiquarian Society at Bournemouth Central Library - who were most helpful, as usual - to find out what it was (corn drying kilns, in case you've forgotten).

The final leg of the Blackmore Vale Path used many more enjoyable paths and tracks, through Bagber and to the Colber bridge, crossing the River Stour into Sturminster Newton. A meandering route then led to Okeford Fitzpaine and over the final escarpment on our return to Blandford Forum. With those stunningly beautiful retrospective views this was a lovely Day's walk but, with the apparently endless, downward sloping return from the top of Okeford Hill to Blandford hastening the end of this fine walk, it was somewhat tinged with sadness. I felt just the same at the end of "The Stour Valley Path" and "The Cranborne Chase Path" so I'm sure that, as soon as I start the next book, I shall become completely besotted with yet another part of Dorset. Fickle, aren't I?

But there is so much to enjoy in Dorset, (but only on foot) it feels as if there's a new adventure waiting around nearly every corner. I must say though, Blackmore Vale is very special and I can't wait to come back again.

Finally, to be boringly technical - the mileages you have covered are:

STAGE 1 - BLANDFORD FORUM TO TOLPUDDLE   13

STAGE 2 - TOLPUDDLE TO DORCHESTER   8.1/2

STAGE 3 - DORCHESTER TO MINTERNE MAGNA   11.1/2

STAGE 4 - MINTERNE MAGNA TO YEOVIL   12.1/4

STAGE 5 - YEOVIL TO STALBRIDGE   12.1/2

STAGE 6 - STALBRIDGE TO BLANDFORD FORUM   13.1/4

TOTAL MILES = 71

THE BLACKMORE VALE PATH

ACKNOWLEDGMENTS

As usual, I have had much assistance from the staff at Bournemouth Reference Library at The Lansdowne. However, as they did not know that they were helping in the production of this masterpiece, I can only assume that this degree of expertise and helpfulness is par for the course. I thank each and every librarian, unreservedly.

I am grateful to John Wilkey, Team Leader for the Rights of Way Section at Dorset County Council, Dorchester for his detailed knowledge of paths, bridleways and other Rights of Way in Dorset, and especially for his assurance that Bradford Hollow (the Cheddar Gorge-like 'County road' which led up from Yeovil to the top Roman kiln lane) is a public route with free access to all - despite the misleading "Dire Consequences to all Trespassers" notice on the top gate. Also, many thanks to Rod Webb, Rights of Way Assistant at Dorchester for investigating the overgrown sections of footpaths/bridleways on the approaches to Tolpuddle, the wired-up gates and other obstructions in the Little Piddle Farm area and other inconveniences which I have added to his work pile. I have also had the usual help from Tom Cook at North Dorset Council who has pointed me in the right direction on several occasions.

Thanks to Fanny Charles at the Blackmore Vale Magazine for her help in determining the 'borders' of the Blackmore Vale, thanks to the very helpful lady who I met at Yeovil Junction for telling me about the chequered history of Barwick House and thanks to the secretary of St Andrew's church, Okeford Fitzpaine for showing me around his lovely church.

Mostly, though, I must thank my wife, Janet who has provided me with sustenance, iced water and endless flasks of coffee during the hottest summer for decades whilst I researched the route and who has put up with my long-term vague communication spells because my head has been full of "The Blackmore Vale Path".

BIBLIOGRAPHY

History and Antiquities of the County of Dorset by Rev John Hutchins

Inventory of Historical Monuments in the County of Dorset: H.M.S.O.

Dorset Churches by Sir Owen Morshead: Dorset Historic Churches Trust

Dorset - Upalong and Downalong by W.I. 1935 members: Ed by Marianne R Dacombe

Proceedings of the Dorset Natural History and Antiquarian Field Club: Ed by Professor J Buckman

Roman Dorset by Bill Putnam: Dovecote Press

Portrait of Dorset by Ralph Wightman: Robert Hale

Chosen Poems of Thomas Hardy: Ed by James Gibson: Macmillan Press

William Barnes by Alan Chedzoy: Dovecote Press

THE BLACKMORE VALE PATH

INDEX

THE BLACKMORE VALE PATH

PERSONAL LOG